FACES OF GRACE

EXPERIENCE THE POWER OF GIVING AND RECEIVING GRACE

An Interactive **30-Day** *Devotional*

Outreach Inc., Vista CA 92081
Outreach.com

ISBN: 978-1-9355-4143-1

Cover and Interior Design: Alexia Wuerdeman
Editorial Services: Snapdragon Group℠, Tulsa, OK

Printed in the United States of America

BECOMING A FACE OF GRACE

I think we all would agree that this journey of life can be extremely complicated, difficult, and troublesome at times. In the midst of overwhelming pressures, intricate relationships, impossible deadlines, and disheartening failures, we long for others to offer us *understanding, forgiveness, a second chance*. We long for grace.

I often tell my people at Calvary Church that I want to be known as a "grace preacher," and that I want our church to be known as a "place of grace." People who have been beaten up by life need a refuge—a place where they will be welcomed warmly, where they can interact with and learn about the love and forgiveness of God, and where compassion flows naturally through people of grace.

Grace is a simple gift that can be difficult to find … and even more challenging to grasp. Here are just a few examples of what grace is:

- God giving us what we need, not what we deserve
- Treating someone with kindness and compassion instead of being critical and judgmental
- Welcoming rather than avoiding
- Seeing the potential in a person rather than seeing their flaws and mistakes
- Practicing patience … especially with loved ones
- Understanding that loving people where they're at often involves risk
- Allowing the love of God to shape you
- The love and forgiveness Jesus Christ offers us on the Cross

The best illustration of grace is obviously found in the person of Christ. If we are living Christ-centered lives, then we need to be living grace-filled lives. Christ did not condemn the woman caught in adultery. He forgave her and then gave her a clear mandate: *Go and sin no more*. (See John 8:11 NLT.) He did not recoil from a demon-possessed man. He lovingly delivered him and then instructed him to bear witness and minister in his community. Christ's character and His actions were driven by His mission: *To seek and to save those who are lost.* (See Luke 19:10 NIV.)

Those of us who follow Christ should be the most grace-filled people around. But far too often, I meet people in the "forgiven" community who seem to have forgotten about the grace they've received. Why is it so easy for us to be critical of others needing the same grace we've received? If we are extending grace to the down-and-out sinner on the street, why can't we extend the same grace to someone in our family who has made poor judgment calls? Why do we celebrate the biblical story of the prodigal son, but shake our heads at the prodigal next door? Why is the Sunday morning worship hour still so highly segregated in some of our communities?

On the Sunday before we began filming *The Grace Card*, we held a commissioning service at Calvary Church, praying for God's hand to be on those involved and on every aspect of the project. During the service, I brought up Taylor Olin, who plays Sam's youngest daughter.

In my hand was a half-filled cup of water. My challenge to Taylor was this: While I held the cup as steady as I could, she would see if she could get any water out of the cup. She could push against my hands, shake my arms, jostle the cup … whatever she could do to spill the water. After a few moments, Taylor was able to send the water flying out of the cup, soaking both of us!

It was a funny moment, and Taylor handled it graciously. I asked the congregation, "Why did water fly all over?" I heard many different responses before someone shouted: "Because there was water in the cup!"

I explained to our people that when things agitate us, when pressures and complexities build, when insults or injury throw us into turmoil, when we are shaken violently—whatever comes out of us is what is in us. If prejudice, hatred, anger, a judgmental spirit, or bitterness comes out, it is only because those things are filling our hearts.

But by the same measure, if *grace*, *love*, and *forgiveness* come out, it's because that is what is housed in our hearts. What's in your heart these days?

When I first heard the story that inspired *The Grace Card*, I was drawn to the character of Sam, a man who is both a pastor and a police sergeant. He seems to have his life together until he encounters Mac, his new partner. Mac's bitterness, anger, prejudice, and attitude make it difficult for Sam (or anyone else) to love him and offer him grace.

Like Sam, we all struggle with loving the hard-to-love. Yet, if we have been the recipient of Christ's lavish grace and forgiveness, we must, in gratitude, strive to extend that same grace to others—even to the difficult people in our lives. Sam's persistence and reliance upon God's strength allows God to use him at a critical time in Mac's life.

Paul writes these words in 1 Corinthians 9:22: "Whatever a person is like, I try to find common ground with him so that he will let me tell him about Christ, and let Christ save him" (TLB).

That is offering grace to others—allowing the love and forgiveness that comes only from Jesus Christ to transform you into a vessel of the Holy Spirit, so that God's grace may flow through you and touch the lives of others. In *The Grace Card*, Grandpa George says, "It's easier to receive grace than it is to give it away." With *Faces of Grace*, our desire is to provide you with thoughtful meditations and challenging stories of how we can take the grace we've been freely given and present it to our fellow man. We all have Macs in our lives. To whom is God calling you to love, forgive, and extend grace?

Our prayer for you, dear reader, is that as you read through these devotionals, as you take time to pray and meditate on the Scriptures that are referenced, as you ponder the stories we have shared, as you ask the Holy Spirit to illuminate and enlighten your mind and heart, that *you* will become one of the Faces of Grace that our society so desperately needs.

Lynn Holmes
Pastor, Calvary Church
Cordova, Tennessee

ACKNOWLEDGMENTS

I want to thank the ministry team at Calvary Church for their heartfelt efforts in creating these devotionals. As a team, we'd like to thank Bob Gordon for his creative efforts and endless energy in editing and compiling this book, and the team at Outreach for their willingness to publish it.

LYNN HOLMES became senior pastor of Calvary Church of the Nazarene in Cordova, Tennessee in 1996, after serving churches in Alabama, Texas, and Oklahoma. "A grace preacher," Pastor Lynn recognizes we all have needs and room for improvement, which is why Christ died for us—to allow us to victoriously deal with life and experience God's grace on a daily basis. Calvary Church, a community-minded fellowship of believers practicing the love and grace of God, is willing to attempt new, cutting-edge ministries, with the movie *The Grace Card,* a prime example of this innovative spirit. Lynn has three children with his late wife, Debbie. Blessed to have remarried, he lives with his wife, Robin, and her two children in Arlington, Tennessee.

MARK HODGE has served as the pastor of worship and arts at Calvary Church since 2003. Through creative services, innovative programs, and special productions, Calvary is a worship center and creative community that welcomes the diverse culture of the greater Memphis area. Mark's wife, Cindy (who plays Dr. Vines in *The Grace Card*), shares his passion for worship and ministry through her leadership and experience in drama and performing arts. The couple has two children.

GREG KENERLY is the connections pastor at Calvary Church, where he has served since 1997. A youth pastor for more than 25 years, Greg served at churches in Florida and Georgia before moving to Memphis. He has been married to his wife, Marlene, since 1987, and they have three children: Corey, Hope, and Kip. Greg enjoys cycling, playing disc golf, hanging out with students, and eating. But mostly, eating.

REV. THOM **MCADORY** serves as the executive pastor at Calvary Church. After receiving his call into ministry while a student at Trevecca Nazarene University, Thom served for 35 years as a music and worship pastor. He most recently served for six years as an adult ministry pastor in Columbia, South Carolina. With more than 40 years of ministry experience and a lifelong passion for Bible teaching, Thom is thoroughly enjoying his responsibilities as executive pastor.

DANIEL **MEDDERS** is the youth pastor at Calvary Church and has served teens in ministry since 2000. Before moving to Memphis to serve at Calvary, he spent four years at a church in central Alabama and five years as part of an inner-city youth ministry in Nashville. Daniel is a graduate of Trevecca Nazarene University and is currently pursuing a Master's degree. He lives near Memphis with his wife, Stefanie, and their two children, Logan and Karlie.

BECKY **MOORE** has been the director of small group ministries at Calvary Church since 2004. Thanks to her experiences in small group Bible studies and seeing the impact these can have in people's lives, she has a passion for God's Word and a desire to see others grow spiritually through this important ministry. In addition, Becky serves on the board of Calvary Pictures. She and her husband, Lynn, have two children, Ben and Hannah.

GREG **NASH** serves as the pastor to families with children at Calvary Church. Greg, whose passion is introducing children to Jesus Christ and teaching them how to live a life of loving God and serving others, has been a children's pastor since 1993. He has a degree in business administration and a Master's in Religion. He and his wife, Denise, have three children: Jim, Jessica, and Jordan. He loves anything to do with the great outdoors.

WES SHAPPLEY is the director of middle school ministries at Calvary Church. He also coaches a middle school basketball team in Memphis. Wes is a student at the University of Memphis, working toward a degree in mathematics with a concentration in secondary education. He hopes to teach high school math and coach basketball, but he's willing to go wherever God leads. He enjoys activities on the lake and playing a variety of sports.

> *Those who have been ransomed by the LORD will return. They will enter Jerusalem singing, crowned with everlasting joy. Sorrow and mourning will disappear, and they will be filled with joy and gladness.*
>
> —Isaiah 35:10 NLT

THE ULTIMATE
FACE OF GRACE

by Lynn Holmes

Life can be hard; all of us recognize that. God has promised the final victory to His followers, but He does not offer a pain-free journey. Life is the training ground for our ultimate eternal home in heaven, but until we get there, we will experience life's ups and downs.

I say this not as a pastor, but as one who has grieved deeply. After twenty-six years of marriage and ministry together, my wife lost a two-year battle with cancer and was called home to heaven. At her funeral service, our church was packed with family, friends, colleagues, parishioners—people with whom we had shared life's journey. They were a great comfort to me, for when I saw each one, my mind flooded with the experiences we had shared. Some memories were of happy times; some were times of working hard together to accomplish a goal; some were times of deep and emotional inspiration and bonding. All provided a welcome moment of relief from my grief. That day, each person was a face of grace to me.

The Bible is straightforward when it talks about the uncertainty of life. One thing is certain: This life is simply the training ground for a better life to follow. While none of God's children, this side of the grave, have seen the beauty and joyous reality of heaven, I believe the Bible gives us some wonderful glimpses. One vision of heaven that intrigues me is that when we make our entrance into that heavenly city—having victoriously finished the race, remained faithful, and endured until the end—there will be a "great crowd of witnesses" cheering our arrival home. (See Hebrews 12:1, NIV.) They will be rejoicing with us as they welcome us to eternal dwelling place.

I believe that as we see each of these welcoming faces, our minds will be flooded with earthly memories of comfort and joy; memories of struggle that ended victoriously; memories of times when we endured, journeyed, and persevered together. Much like the reminders I saw at my late wife's funeral, these faces of grace will illuminate what God enabled us to do through Him.

I also believe there will be one face our hearts will long to see above every other: a face that we never saw visibly in this life, but one that will be immediately recognizable. That's because throughout this entire journey, He was that one who "sticks closer than a brother." (See Proverbs 18:24 NIV.) He was that one who would "never leave us nor forsake us." (See Hebrews 13:5 NIV.) His presence through all of life's ups and downs enabled us

TAKE A STAND

Life can wear you down. Read through these passages when you need an encouraging reminder that our ultimate victory is assured through Jesus Christ:

Isaiah 35, 2 Peter 1:11, Revelation 21:1–5, Isaiah 65:17–25

to persevere and find an inner strength that was not our own. In the moment we see Him for the first time, His face will radiate with grace. All of life's sorrow and mourning will disappear, and we will be filled with eternal joy and gladness!

With every breath I take in this life, I am getting closer to that grand entrance into my heavenly home, where I will have the awesome privilege of seeing my Lord *face to face*. I believe I will experience unfathomable peace, contentment, and happiness. I will know the feeling of incredible fulfillment, victory, and assurance. I will be overwhelmed as I look upon the *ultimate face of grace*: Jesus Christ, my Lord!

SCRIPTURE
TO REMEMBER

Therefore, since we are surrounded by such a great cloud of witnesses, let us throw off everything that hinders and the sin that so easily entangles, and let us run with perseverance the race marked out for us. Let us fix our eyes on Jesus, the author and perfecter of our faith, who for the joy set before him endured the cross, scorning its shame, and sat down at the right hand of the throne of God. Consider him who endured such opposition from sinful men, so that you will not grow weary and lose heart.

—Hebrews 12:1–3 NIV

de•fin•ing moment
THE GREEK WORD TRANSLATED "WITNESSES" IN HEBREWS 12:1 IS THE ORIGIN OF OUR ENGLISH WORD "MARTYR." IT MEANS: "TESTIFIERS, WITNESSES." IT REFERENCES THOSE WHO ARE BEARING TESTIMONY TO THE POWER OF FAITH AND GOD'S FAITHFULNESS.

Do you know someone who is struggling with life's difficulties? Write the person's name below and list some ways you can show support.

_____

_____

_____

_____

_____

_____

_____

_____

_____

_____

_____

_____

_____

_____

_____

_____

_____

_____

_____

_____

_____

_____

> When Judas, who had betrayed him, saw that Jesus was condemned, he was seized with remorse and returned the thirty silver coins to the chief priests and the elders.
>
> —Matthew 27:3 NIV

THE PRICE
OF GUILT

by Daniel Medders

Can I be honest with you? When I was a young boy, I was punished often. Can I be even more honest with you? I deserved more punishment than I ever received! When I was given a rule, I always wanted to know how bad the punishment would be so I could decide whether or not the rule was worth breaking. Some forms of punishment were way worse than others—especially being sent to bed early or being grounded from fishing. Anything else, I could handle.

But losing out on a meal or fishing time was nothing compared to the worst punishment I ever received. I don't recall what I did, but I do remember vividly what happened afterward. I was sitting on my bed when my father walked in. He wasn't angry, but he sure wasn't happy. I remember him sitting down beside me with a look of disgust. "Son," he said, "I just don't know what to do with you anymore. I'm just so disappointed in you."

Let me tell you, I would rather have been forced to give away all of my fishing equipment than to hear that phrase. I felt as if I had been torn apart inside. I could handle my dad being angry or frustrated with me, but in that one instance, I felt as if I had caused my dad to give up on me. What a terrible feeling. I felt like I had betrayed my father.

Jesus knew what it was like to be betrayed. Have you ever wondered why Judas was so willing to betray Jesus? Some say Judas did it for the money—but most scholars point out that the 30 pieces of silver he received was the normal "going rate" for a slave in those days. So it seems unlikely that Judas would have been motivated by an average transaction fee—especially in light of the potential bounty the leaders might have eventually put on Jesus' head.

Whatever drove him to sell Jesus, we read in Matthew 27 that Judas realized his disastrous mistake and tried to give the money back. Can you imagine the guilt that Judas must have felt? It became apparent to all when Judas hung himself. His guilt was overwhelming.

As my dad sat on my bed, I knew a similarly overwhelming feeling. I imagine all of us, at some point, have had heartbreaking reactions when we let down those who love us. The power of guilt can be overbearing, keeping us up at night, destroying our confidence, stopping us from enjoying life. There are many ways to handle guilt: Some ignore it and act like the mistake never occurred; some blame others. Unfortunately, some, like Judas, can never overcome the guilt.

How would God have us deal with guilt? By seeking forgiveness, both from God and from those we have hurt. Maybe you have something in your life that requires you to ask for forgiveness. I knew sitting on my bed that day that I needed to apologize to my dad. It wasn't easy, but it sure beat the alternative: feelings of guilt that would have hounded me. Of all the ways we have to deal with guilt, resolution and repentance is always the best possible option.

SCRIPTURE
TO REMEMBER

Then Satan entered Judas, called Iscariot, one of the Twelve. And Judas went to the chief priests and the officers of the temple guard and discussed with them how he might betray Jesus. They were delighted and agreed to give him money. He consented, and watched for an opportunity to hand Jesus over to them when no crowd was present.

—Luke 22:3–6 NIV

de•fin•ing moment

GUILT: "A FEELING OF RESPONSIBILITY OR REMORSE FOR SOME OFFENSE, CRIME, WRONG, ETC., WHETHER REAL OR IMAGINED."

REPENTANCE: "DEEP SORROW, COMPUNCTION, OR CONTRITION FOR A PAST SIN, WRONGDOING, OR THE LIKE."

" QUOTE, UNQUOTE "

You will certainly carry out God's purpose, however you act, but it makes a difference to you whether you serve like Judas or like John.

—C.S. Lewis

List the negative consequences of the guilt you feel from a mistake. If possible, make amends. If not, think through ways to avoid similar guilt-inducing situations.

CARDBOARD
GRACE

by Wes Shappley

Easter Sunday, along with Christmas, is a day when many people feel an obligation to go to church. The men wear their nicest suits, and the ladies wear their biggest hats and fanciest dresses. It's a wonderful opportunity for the church to reach out to people who don't regularly attend, but who are open (at least for one day) to the message of grace and forgiveness.

One Easter, our church decided to incorporate cardboard testimonies into our service. These brief testimonies are a visually powerful worship element. A group of people stands at the front of the church, each person holding a piece of cardboard. Something is written on the front side of the cardboard, like: "Was strung out on drugs." The person then turns the cardboard over for the rest of their story, like: "Now I'm transformed, clean, and forgiven!"

I was extremely excited when I was asked to present my cardboard testimony to the church that Easter. Until I realized I didn't know what my story would be. Most of the cardboard testimonies I had seen were dramatic: people who had overcome abuse, suffered the tragic loss of a loved one, or been involved in a serious accident. I was thankful that those are not issues from my past.

But because I didn't have a dramatic life-change story, I began to wonder if I was worthy of this opportunity. A week before Easter, I still didn't have my cardboard prepared. When my youth pastor asked me what my testimony would say, I told him that I wasn't sure, to which he responded, "I have it! On one side, say: My youth pastor thought I would end up in jail. On the other side, say: But now I'm a youth leader!"

There's nothing like the encouragement of a good friend, right? But we all know there has to be some truth in humor or it wouldn't be funny. Here's the truth he was referring to.

I'm the fourth generation of my family to worship at our church. I was in church all the time when I was growing up, but that didn't mean I was perfect. In fact, around church I was known as "a holy terror." My mother was my kindergarten Sunday school teacher, and she had to get my dad to come sit in class to keep me under control for her to teach. I was wild, loud, and mean when I was younger, disobedient, disrespectful, and a bully as I grew older.

I changed dramatically during a summer mission trip when I was thirteen. God gave me an understanding of His love that washed away all of my sins and created me new again. God's grace became real, and it was enough for me.

Suddenly, I realized that while my youth pastor was joking, he had actually crafted the perfect cardboard testimony for me. As I read other testimonies that Easter, I realized that no matter what your life has been like and no matter whether your life change has been "big" or "small," God's grace in your life can be used to touch others.

The dramatic (and not so dramatic) stories of changed lives that were told on those pieces of cardboard touched everyone who came to our church that Easter. Each and every story highlighted one thing: By the grace of God, we can overcome our sins, our pain, and our past. And when we do, our testimonies can extend that same grace to help others overcome whatever issues they have.

SCRIPTURE
TO REMEMBER

While they were going out, a man who was demon-possessed and could not talk was brought to Jesus. And when the demon was driven out, the man who had been mute spoke. The crowd was amazed and said, "Nothing like this has ever been seen in Israel."

—Matthew 9:32–33 NIV

QUOTE, UNQUOTE

Amazing grace, how sweet the sound,
That saved a wretch like me.
I once was lost, but now am found,
Was blind, but now I see.

—*John Newton, Amazing Grace*

Take time to write out your testimony, and then condense it into two lines. The first should tell about what you used to deal with (or be like). The second should be about what God has done to rescue you.

_____

_____

_____

_____

_____

_____

_____

_____

_____

_____

_____

_____

TODAY'S PRAYER

Lord, thank You for the testimony You have given me to share. My life would be meaningless without You. With You, I have everything I need—both for this life and throughout eternity. Thank You for sending Jesus Christ to be the sacrifice for our sins so that we could be reconciled with You, regardless of what we may have done in the past. Your grace is nothing short of amazing.

It's in Jesus' wonderful name I pray. Amen.

> *For it is by grace you have been saved, through faith—and this not from yourselves, it is the gift of God— not by works, so that no one can boast.*
>
> —Ephesians 2:8–9 NIV

IT'S
FREE!

by Greg Nash

Free!

That's always an eye-catching word, isn't it? Free is something that *always* grabs my attention. Of course, it might not hold my attention for long after I see what is being given away—especially if we're talking free kittens, free car insurance quotes, or free advice. Still, free always makes me look—because I like free! And nothing says free like a grand opening—they give away all kinds of free stuff, and they usually throw in free food, as well.

While there is something captivating about free, I am, like most people, somewhat wary of it. I always check the fine print on any free offer because a lot of times there are strings attached and hidden charges. Free has been abused in our society, causing us to not fully trust it.

Maybe that is why so many of us struggle with this Scripture passage in Ephesians 2. We discover that grace is a gift of

God—but what about the fine print? As a child in Sunday school, I learned that grace is "a good gift that we don't deserve." According to the Apostle Paul, all that we have to do is believe—and accept it—by faith.

But what, you might be asking, is in the fine print? You might be thinking this sounds too good to be true, and we've all heard that if something sounds too good to be true, it probably is. So it's understandably hard for some of us to believe that God would give us—the undeserving wretches that we are—salvation from sin and death. All for free!

Maybe that's why Paul made sure to add "not by works." In this case, the fine print actually *helps* us, showing that free actually means free. There are those who think that something so valuable—God's grace—can't be free, so we must earn it by doing good works in exchange for our salvation. But there is nothing we can do or need to do to earn it.

Paul goes on to say that if we could earn our salvation, then we likely would boast about what we had accomplished. But salvation is not about our works. It's all about what Christ has accomplished by dying on the Cross to make our salvation possible. →

CHECK LIST

Here are three questions for you to ponder about the free gift of grace:

☐ 1) Why do you think God has made salvation a free gift instead of asking us to do something to earn it?

☐ 2) Do you ever struggle with the fact that God's grace is free and there's nothing you can do to earn it?

☐ 3) Have you accepted God's gift of salvation?

A little girl I know was struggling to play a musical instrument. In the year she had been taking lessons, she hadn't really progressed, and she wasn't having much fun. When I asked her why she kept playing, she replied, "If I become good at this, it might get my daddy's attention and then maybe he'll be proud of me and love me."

Wow. Think about *that*. I am thankful that our heavenly Father loves us so much that we don't have to try to win His approval and affection. His wonderful gift of salvation is just that: a gift. If you have accepted this gift, live like it by sharing grace, not working like you're having to continually earn it. If you haven't done so yet, accept God's gift today. It's free! But be sure to read the fine print. You are signing on to a loving relationship with Almighty God for now and all of eternity.

How's that for free?

SCRIPTURE
TO REMEMBER

Like the rest, we were by nature objects of wrath. But because of his great love for us, God, who is rich in mercy, made us alive with Christ even when we were dead in transgressions—it is by grace you have been saved. And God raised us up with Christ and seated us with him in the heavenly realms in Christ Jesus, in order that in the coming ages he might show the incomparable riches of his grace, expressed in his kindness to us in Christ Jesus.

—Ephesians 2:3b–7 NIV

de•fin•ing moment

SALVATION: "DELIVERANCE FROM THE POWER AND PENALTY OF SIN; REDEMPTION."

What was your reaction to the story about the little girl trying to earn her daddy's attention and affection? How does it mirror or oppose your image of your own heavenly Father?

_____

_____

_____

_____

_____

_____

_____

_____

_____

_____

_____

_____

_____

_____

_____

_____

_____

_____

_____

_____

_____

_____

> *"Let's have a feast and celebrate.*
> *For this son of mine was dead and is alive again;*
> *he was lost and is found."*
>
> —Luke 15:23b-24a NIV

PRICELESS

by Mark Hodge

An avid fisherman, my father-in-law never missed an opportunity to pull out his boat and gear and head out on the lake with his long-time fishing buddy. One summer day, they had been on the water without a single catch when Dad felt that familiar tug on his fishing line. He sprang into action with more than a little pride, sensing that he was about to land the only catch of the day, thanks to his favorite lure.

Dad was reeling in the line when an extremely large heron swooped down from fifty feet behind the boat and swiped his catch. The bird soared off with the fish in its beak, and the fishing line trailing behind. Dad quickly turned the boat around and released his reel so the bird could take the line. The heron headed for the bank and landed several yards from the shore, before disappearing into the woods with the fish.

Dad quickly realized he had a decision to make. That was, after all, *his* fish and not the heron's. As if it wasn't bad enough to lose the lone catch of the day, his favorite—and most expensive—lure was still in the mouth of *his* fish. The only way to access *his* fish and retrieve *his* lure would be to go into the woods after them.

While his friend helmed the boat, Dad stepped onto the bank and started following his line into the woods. He had walked about one hundred fifty feet before he spotted the bird with *his* fish and *his* lure. The heron, not interested in a confrontation, heard Dad thrashing around, dropped the fish, and flew off. With fish and lure in hand, Dad returned to the boat, victorious. He and his buddy returned to the house with one fish and one whale of a story!

Not being a fisherman, I can never fully grasp Dad's decision to take on a heron, but I know there wasn't even a split second of hesitation in his decision. Would he have gone to such lengths to recover one of his other, less expensive lures? Highly unlikely. Would he have chased that heron into the woods if he and his buddy had already caught a dozen or more fish that day? Of course not. But when there is only one fish to show for a day of fishing, and that fish is stolen right out from under you, taking your best lure with it, your response is bound to be different.

In that moment, the lure and the fish were priceless in his eyes. I don't have to be a fisherman to appreciate Dad's determination. Each of us invests fully and consistently in that which is most important to us. Whatever it is that we value or cherish, we count the cost and set out after it. We spare no expense in the pursuit.

That's what God does too—only more so. His greatest treasure? Each and every one of us. We are what He holds most dearly. As we are reminded in 1 Corinthians 6:19b–20a, "You are not your own; you were bought at a price" (NIV). Through His Son, Jesus Christ, God has paid the ultimate price for us, and He is determined to capture us with His grace. Constantly pursued and unconditionally loved. We are priceless.

SCRIPTURE
TO REMEMBER

"Again, the kingdom of heaven is like a merchant looking for fine pearls. When he found one of great value, he went away and sold everything he had and bought it."

—Matthew 13:45–46 NIV

"If a man owns a hundred sheep, and one of them wanders away, will he not leave the ninety-nine on the hills and go to look for the one that wandered off? And if he finds it, I tell you the truth, he is happier about that one sheep than about the ninety-nine that did not wander off."

—Matthew 18:12b–13 NIV

de•fin•ing moment

TREASURE: "WEALTH OR RICHES STORED OR ACCUMULATED, ESPECIALLY IN THE FORM OF PRECIOUS METALS, MONEY, JEWELS, OR PLATE; ANY THING OR PERSON GREATLY VALUED OR HIGHLY PRIZED."

What are the five most important things in your life? Do your daily choices reflect what you value most?

_____

_____

_____

_____

_____

_____

_____

_____

_____

_____

_____

_____

TODAY'S PRAYER

Dear Lord, thank You for Your everlasting love. Thank You for treasuring me so much that You gave Your life for me. I am unable to comprehend the price You willingly paid. Remind me today that every person I interact with is a great treasure in Your eyes, and help me see each of them through Your eyes.

In Jesus' name, amen.

> "The King will reply, 'I tell you the truth, whatever you did for one of the least of these brothers of mine, you did for me'."
>
> —Matthew 25:40 NIV

LUNCH
WITH JESUS

by Greg Kenerly

As a youth pastor, I really enjoy meeting students for lunch at their schools. It's a great way to see them in their environment and meet their friends. One such visit remains powerfully etched in my memory: the day I ate with David, who is an active member of our ministry and popular among his peers.

While there rarely is assigned seating in a high school cafeteria, students tend to sit in the same place with the same people every day. It's fairly easy to tell what activities students are involved in based on what group they sit with. You see band students together, ROTC members together, football players together, and so on.

At David's school, the majority of kids sit in rows of long tables in the middle of the cafeteria. I noticed there were also some small round tables on the sides of the cafeteria that were not heavily utilized. The ones that were mostly had just one person at them. I quickly surmised that students without a group to call their own were at these tables. These were the kids who are often labeled by their peers as loners, outcasts, or worse, "rejects."

As I waited for David, I found the area where I thought we would be sitting based on the group that was already seated there. Among them was a student David had recently brought to our church. To my surprise, however, David led me to one of the little round tables at the side of the cafeteria. He introduced me to a girl named Stephanie before he headed off to grab some food.

I sensed immediately that Stephanie was not a part of David's normal "group." She was likely not part of any group. After meeting me, Stephanie began talking about how much she hated school. She hated riding the bus. She hated her classes. She hated the teachers. By this time, I was really hoping David was in the "express" lane and would be back at the table soon!

I sat there and nodded my head as Stephanie unloaded about all the things she hated. She told me no one at the school liked her—except David. No one ever talked to her—except David. →

CHECK LIST

Here are three great verses to remind you to be kind and loving:

☐ 1) "Do to others as you would have them do to you." Luke 6:31 NIV

☐ 2) Be kind and compassionate to one another, forgiving each other, just as in Christ God forgave you. Ephesians 4:32 NIV

☐ 3) Dear children, let's not merely say that we love each other; let us show the truth by our actions. 1 John 3:18 NLT

No one ever sat with her at lunch—except David. It quickly became apparent that David made it a point to be Stephanie's friend because no one else was. As I left the school and walked back to my car, a smile broke across my face. I realized that even though it looked like David across the table, I had actually just eaten lunch with Jesus.

When I later asked David about his friend Stephanie, he told me that he noticed her sitting by herself day after day while he sat with his group of friends. "I felt like Jesus was saying she needed a friend, so I went and sat with her one day, and I've been there ever since."

One thing I know as a youth pastor is that there are a great many "Stephanies" in our schools—and in our workplaces, as well. People are often alone, even in a crowded room. What would our world look like if we were more like David when we cross paths with a Stephanie? Maybe we should find out.

" QUOTE, UNQUOTE "

Until further notice, be nice to everyone.

—Wisdom found under the lid of a soft drink

TODAY'S PRAYER

Lord, thank You for the freedom that comes from forgiveness. Please show me where I have let my pride enslave me in bitterness or anger toward others. Direct me to the people to whom I need to extend forgiveness and help me to ask humbly for their forgiveness. Please help me display your grace through all my relationships. In Jesus' name, amen.

Is there someone in your life that could use a friend? Write down some ways you can be Jesus to that person by reaching out to them.

And, in their prayers for you their hearts will go out to you, because of the surpassing grace God has given you.

—2 Corinthians 9:14 NIV

PRAYING
FOR CHANGE

by Becky Moore

At my first job in the computer industry, I worked with a guy named Andrew. It didn't take me long to realize we had nothing in common. In addition to having different religious views, I considered him to be immature, loud, and obnoxious. In fact, Andrew made my work environment miserable. I tried to ignore him, but instead, I often became rude and impatient with him. After a while, I began feeling terrible for harboring bad thoughts about him.

You see, I knew Andrew didn't deserve this kind of treatment, especially from someone who is a follower of Christ. He really never did anything wrong. I just couldn't stand him, his personality, or his religious beliefs!

One day, God impressed on me the responsibility I had to pray for Andrew. Honestly, I didn't want to pray for him, but I did it out of obedience. Needless to say, my prayers for Andrew were anything but genuine at first. They really centered on me and my ability to tolerate him at work. However, over time, I realized I was becoming a little more caring and sincere in my prayers. It wasn't long before they were heartfelt and completely centered on God's blessing on Andrew's life.

What was the difference? God used my prayer time to change me, not Andrew. He was the same guy, but God had allowed me to see him differently—as He sees him. My heart became sensitive to Andrew because I knew God loved and cared for him. Eventually, I considered Andrew to be more than just a coworker. He had become my friend. God took my wrong motives for wanting to pray for Andrew and replaced them with caring feelings for him instead. When he was married later that year, I wished him the best and prayed for his new wife and their marriage.

The Apostle Paul recognized the relational impact of prayer. In 2 Corinthians, we learn that the Gentiles from the Corinthian church had donated an offering to help the Jewish Christians in Jerusalem. Paul knew that as the Jewish recipients prayed in gratitude, their hearts would "go out to" the contributing Gentiles. One of the benefits to prayer is that it brings us closer in our relationships to the ones for whom we are praying.

As you pray for people, your heart can't help but become more warm and loving toward them. Paul realized that as the Jewish Christians prayed, they would have a deeper understanding of God's grace extended to the Gentiles and fully accept them as fellow believers in Christ Jesus. Because of prayer, the unity among the Jewish and Gentile believers would be strengthened. →

CHECK LIST

If you're wrestling with praying for someone you might not like, here are three benefits:

☐ You will be obedient to God's call.

☐ It takes the focus of your prayers off you.

☐ God will change your heart in regard to that person.

In *The Grace Card*, Sam had conflicting feelings for Mac. As a Christian and a pastor, Sam knew he should love Mac unconditionally … but Mac had a way of bringing out the worst feelings hidden deep inside Sam's heart. When Mac was faced with a terrible crisis, Sam felt helpless but prayed earnestly for Mac. Sam had no idea that God would soften his heart to the place where he could step in to serve Mac and his family. God's grace through prayer changed Sam's heart and attitude.

It's nearly impossible to pray for someone and still hold on to bad feelings toward them. Prayer might not change the person for whom we are praying—that's God's job. Our job is to pray and discover how God is changing us!

QUESTION

?

OF THE DAY

WHEN SOMEONE ANNOYS YOU, IS YOUR FIRST RESPONSE TO PRAY FOR THEM OR COMPLAIN ABOUT THEM?

_____

_____

"" QUOTE, UNQUOTE ,,

It is not so true that "prayer changes things" as that prayer changes me and I change things. God has so constituted things that prayer on the basis of Redemption alters the way in which a man looks at things. Prayer is not a question of altering things externally, but of working wonders in a man's disposition.

—Oswald Chambers

Write out a prayer for a person to whom you need to extend grace.

_____

_____

_____

_____

_____

_____

_____

_____

_____

_____

_____

_____

_____

_____

_____

_____

_____

_____

_____

_____

_____

In everything, by prayer and petition, with thanksgiving, present your requests to God.

—Philippians 4:6b NIV

I PROMISE
TO PRAY FOR YOU

by Thom McAdory

I worked for a number of years with a pastor who loved to tell our congregation that "the very best thing you can do for someone is to pray for them." A favorite query of another pastor friend is "How can I pray for you?" It's even printed on his business card. But this is no catch phrase to him; he means it. He prays regularly for people.

I have often told folks I'd pray for them and have done just that. Sometimes though, I've made that promise only to realize later I hadn't prayed. When the Lord reminds me of those commitments, I begin praying, first out of guilt, but then out of desire. I'm thankful God allows us to participate in praying for others. As Paul challenges us in Ephesians 6:18, we should "be alert and always keep on praying for all the saints" (NIV). That's how I want to live.

An odd thing I've noticed about praying: There's a correlation between how much we pray and how much we desire to pray. The less I pray, the less often the idea of praying comes to mind. The more I pray, the more I desire to do so. Maybe that's why I

Thessalonians 5:17 exhorts us to "pray continually" (NIV).

I believe that prayer changes things—with a key change occurring in me *as* I pray. My attitude toward someone I'm praying for takes on a whole new look. I not only want to talk to God about that person, but I also feel genuinely invested in their wellbeing. My prayer for you turns out to be good not only for you, but also for me.

If praying for someone is easier for you to say than to do, here are some ideas to keep you focused on your promise:

You may need to pray for yourself first to be prepared to pray for others. "The prayer of a righteous man is powerful and effective" (James 5:16b NIV).

Pray immediately after you've promised to pray. "And pray in the Spirit on all occasions with all kinds of prayers and requests" (Ephesians 6:18a NIV).

Pray for your friend to be open to the work of God even if it is not the answer he or she may want.

Pray for God's presence even though it may seem that nothing is happening. Remember: God is *always* at work.

Pray for the understanding that in reality, God *is* the answer to your prayer. "If you then, though you are evil, know how to give good gifts to your children, how much more will your Father in heaven give the Holy Spirit to those who ask him!" (Luke 11:13 NIV).

Keep what you're praying about between you, your friend, and God, unless the person you are praying for asks you to share their need with someone else.

When the Lord brings your friend to mind, pray then and there, making the most of your reminder!

Find a set time each day to pray for your friend.

Allow God to lead your prayer time. He will help you know what to pray.

Perhaps most importantly, believe that God is concerned about your friend even more than you are, and He can do "… immeasurably more than all we ask or imagine, according to his power that is at work within us" (Ephesians 3:20 NIV).

So, my friend, I promise to pray for you. And I trust God to bring you to mind in order that I can do just that.

SCRIPTURE
TO REMEMBER

In the same way, the Spirit helps us in our weakness. We do not know what we ought to pray for, but the Spirit himself intercedes for us with groans that words cannot express. And he who searches our hearts knows the mind of the Spirit, because the Spirit intercedes for the saints in accordance with God's will.

—Romans 8:26–27 NIV

" QUOTE, UNQUOTE "

To be a Christian without prayer is no more possible than to be alive without breathing.

—Dr. Martin Luther King, Jr.

When we offer to pray for another person, it isn't because we're experts, it's because we know God hears our prayers. What usually happens when you say, "I'll pray for you"?

_____
_____
_____
_____
_____
_____
_____
_____
_____
_____

TODAY'S PRAYER

Dear Lord, forgive me for the times I tell a friend that I will pray for them and then forget to do so. Thank You for the privilege of coming to You with the needs of my friends and family. Help me to cherish the opportunity to pray for people and help me to remember to do so regularly. Thanks for being a God who hears our prayers. And thank You for the opportunity to pray.

In Jesus' name, amen.

> *For God was in Christ, reconciling the world to himself, no longer counting people's sins against them. And he gave us this wonderful message of reconciliation. So we are Christ's ambassadors; God is making his appeal through us.*
>
> —2 Corinthians 5:19–20a NLT

AMBASSADORS
OF GRACE

by Lynn Holmes

Want to follow Christ? Want others to see His love shining through you? Grace is the essential ingredient that must consume, characterize, and control *every* aspect of your life. Grace must transform who you are and how you see others. You must live, walk, and breathe grace. For not only are you the recipient of grace, you must also be a messenger of grace in gratitude and response. Paul refers to this as being "Christ's ambassadors." When you are an ambassador, your actions speak as loudly as your words. It's not easy, but it is your responsibility.

I read of a man named Charles, who had new neighbors move in next door. He introduced himself and welcomed them to the neighborhood. Before he left, he invited them to attend his church. The father responded to Charles with a "Thanks, but no thanks." But he didn't stop there: "I don't understand how anybody in their right mind could be a Christian. I don't see how anybody with any intelligence could believe in religion. It is for weaklings and people who do not have enough sense to think for themselves." And with that, Charles's new neighbor shut the door—both literally and figuratively.

It's interesting to me that the neighbor's argument boils down to this: *Christianity is for cowards.* It takes enormous courage just to become a Christian and immense boldness, strength, and confidence to take a stand for Christ in this world. Great people never follow the crowd; they take the road less traveled. Offering grace to another individual is an act of gratitude for what Christ has done for us, and an act of worship and allegiance to Christ. He has given us His wonderful message of reconciliation, and sharing that message is the gracious—and courageous—thing to do.

When we allow grace to characterize and control our every waking moment, God opens up opportunities to extend that same grace to others. Yet while those opportunities will be there, it takes courage to share grace. I believe that many Christians are afraid to take a stand for Christ because they don't want to be labeled as "narrow-minded" or "old-fashioned". It's uncomfortable to hold people accountable. It is difficult to challenge other people's erroneous ways of living for fear of being accused of judgmentalism.

That brings us back to Charles. He knew that extending grace to his neighbor was going to take courage, so he asked God for help … and to provide an opportunity. Several weeks later, Charles noticed his neighbor's rain gutters were filled with leaves. As he was wondering why his neighbor had not cleaned out his gutters, the neighbor's wife walked outside. So Charles asked her about the gutters. "My husband won't climb up there to clean them out because he is deathly afraid of heights." Suddenly, Charles felt that inner nudge of the Holy Spirit. He went into his garage, grabbed his ladder, and promptly cleaned out his neighbor's rain gutters. That one act of kindness opened up a door for the beginning of a relationship. Nothing in the heart of Charles's neighbor changed overnight, but today, years later, his neighbors are leaders in the church that they attend with Charles.

We will find opportunities to present grace to people in our world if we listen to the still, small voice of God. As ambassadors, we represent our Savior every minute of the day. And as *ambassadors with courage*, we care more about the things of God than the things of this world.

SCRIPTURE
TO REMEMBER

"This is my command—be strong and courageous! Do not be afraid or discouraged. For the LORD your God is with you wherever you go."

—Joshua 1:9 NLT

Take courage, for the coming of the Lord is near.

—James 5:8 TLB

Having hope will give you courage.

—Job 11:18a NLT

" QUOTE, UNQUOTE "

An ambassador has no need of spies; his character is always sacred.

— George Washington

Who do you know who could benefit from hearing about God's grace? Write the person's name below, along with some ideas for talking to that person about Jesus.

_____

_____

_____

_____

_____

_____

_____

_____

_____

_____

TODAY'S PRAYER

Dear Lord, thank You for choosing me to be Your ambassador. Forgive me for the times I have not chosen to be courageous when I've had the opportunity to share Your grace, even though I know so many desperately need it. Please help me remember to listen for those inner nudges from the Holy Spirit when opportunities are presented. And please help me to remember that I represent You everywhere I go.

In Jesus' name I pray. Amen.

REACHING OUT
GRACEFULLY

by Daniel Medders

Several years ago, I served on the governing board of a small retreat and conference center. One fellow member was Roy, whom I can best describe as a hymn-singing, King James-reading, suit-and-tie-wearing, old-school Christian. I mean no harm if that describes you, as well. It was just that I, on the other hand, wore jeans, untucked shirts, flip-flops, and sunglasses atop my head—all obvious signs of a hip Christian! Roy and I could not have been any more different in my eyes—or in his.

That became obvious during the course of one board meeting. Roy talked negatively about the way the center's youth leadership was carrying out their ministry objectives. As a youth pastor involved in that program, I took his critique personally; my response was less than calm and reasoned. By the end of the discussion, Roy had concluded I wasn't a hip Christian at all. He felt I was an arrogant young punk, while I was certain he was completely out of touch. When we left that day, I would have been fine never interacting with Roy again. Oh, the joys of serving in ministry together.

Under the circumstances, you would think I'd have been pleased to learn soon after this encounter that Roy had resigned from the board to move back to his hometown. One slight problem: Roy was moving back to *my* town and *my* church—the place where I served as the youth pastor. The man who had attacked my hard work at the retreat center would now be sitting in the same pews as me every Sunday.

My way of dealing with this was exactly what you would expect from any ordained minister—I decided I would avoid him. I did all I could to make sure our paths didn't cross. Months of success followed … except for that gnawing conviction that I tried valiantly to ignore. One day as I prayed, I sensed God was telling me to meet with Roy. Reluctantly, I called and asked him to join me for lunch. With what sounded like equal reluctance, he accepted my invitation.

I learned a lot about Roy that day. Like all of us, he has an interesting story. His driving motivation in life was to ensure that the message of Jesus Christ would never be watered down—so he wasn't going to let it happen on his watch. What I saw as my creative ministry, he saw as a threat to God's message.

By the end of a meaningful lunch, we each asked for and offered forgiveness. Roy and I still do not dress the same, nor do we hold the same vision for the church. But despite our differences,

TAKE A STAND

Two mission-minded Christians named Paul and Barnabas had such a strong disagreement that they parted ways. Chances are that kind of disagreement has occurred in your life. Pray for ways you can reestablish any broken relationships that resulted. And then do what it takes to set things right!

I respect Roy for his great passion for Christ. Roy and I greet each other with smiles and shake hands every Sunday. When I announced I would be moving to a new church, Roy told me he would miss me. Roy, like me, is a passionate man for the Gospel. We may not hold many of the same philosophies, but I do aspire to have his enthusiasm and zeal as I grow older.

Roy and I have definitely come a long way since that board meeting where we were both convinced we knew God's will, despite being on different sides. When I finally discovered God's will a few months later, it turned out that God wanted me to extend grace to Roy and restart the relationship, without the prejudices I had originally entertained. I am better for having done so.

SCRIPTURE
TO REMEMBER

Paul said to Barnabas, "Let us go back and visit the brothers in all the towns where we preached the word of the Lord and see how they are doing." Barnabas wanted to take John, also called Mark, with them, but Paul did not think it wise to take him, because he had deserted them in Pamphylia and had not continued with them in the work. They had such a sharp disagreement that they parted company.

—Acts 15:36–39 NIV

QUOTE, UNQUOTE

To disagree, one doesn't have to be disagreeable.

—Barry Goldwater

Relive a disagreement that ended a relationship.
What lessons did you learn that you can apply
to future relationships?

GRACE IS A
SECOND CHANCE

by Greg Nash

My friend Donna grew up in the church, but when she reached her late teens, she decided she had had enough. She stopped attending and allowed bad company and bad habits to lead her farther and farther away from God. Through it all, her mother persistently prayed for and loved her.

On special occasions like Easter and Christmas, Donna usually agreed to attend church with her family, but that was the extent of it. The folks in our church were always kind and loving when she was here, letting her know she was missed. Even though she felt loved at church, Donna also felt convicted about the life she was living. She didn't want to deal with those feelings, so it was easier just to stay away.

Finally, when Donna was closing in on forty, she gave in to her mother's pleadings and began attending church somewhat regularly. Donna's habits and lifestyle had not changed much, but her mom saw coming to church as a good first step.

About that same time, I was beginning to recruit workers for a new midweek children's ministry program. As I thought through and prayed about potential teachers, Donna's name kept coming to my mind. But I also knew she was not living a Christ-like life, and our church had policies requiring people in leadership positions to set godly examples.

Still, I could not get away from the thought of Donna at least helping out in the program. Finally after the senior pastor and I talked and prayed, we decided that we would extend grace to Donna by asking her to be a classroom assistant. To the surprise of many, Donna accepted.

In Luke 19, we read about Zacchaeus, a man who made his living at the expense of others. But while those people despised him, Jesus loved him; he saw Zacchaeus's unlimited potential. When Jesus called out to him, Zacchaeus immediately began following Jesus and made it a point to pay back those he had wronged. Much like Zacchaeus, Donna needed a second chance.

Over the next few weeks, we watched as Donna blossomed, faithfully serving and loving the children in her class. She began to rethink her life, and one Sunday morning at the end of the service, Donna made her way to the front of the sanctuary where she knelt at an altar to pray.

Others came alongside to pray for and support her. When asked for her prayer needs, Donna replied, "How can I keep working with the children and be a godly example for them if I'm not living

TAKE A STAND

Consider volunteering in a local ministry that serves the many people who are desperate for a second chance. This might be a prison ministry, homeless shelter, or crisis pregnancy center. Look for an opportunity to share the love of the God of second chances.

for God? I need to make things right with Him." Years of prayers by her mother and her friends were answered in that moment.

We all know people like Donna who have walked away from their relationship with God and then are not sure if God will take them back. They question how God could ever forgive them for all they have done contrary to His will. Sometimes, it takes another person believing in them, seeing their worth, offering a little grace, and giving them a second chance to realize that our loving heavenly Father is a God of second chances.

SCRIPTURE
TO REMEMBER

When Jesus reached the spot, he looked up and said to him, "Zacchaeus, come down immediately. I must stay at your house today." So he came down at once and welcomed him gladly. All the people saw this and began to mutter, "He has gone to be the guest of a 'sinner'." But Zacchaeus stood up and said to the Lord, "Look, Lord! Here and now I give half of my possessions to the poor, and if I have cheated anybody out of anything, I will pay back four times the amount." Jesus said to him, "Today salvation has come to this house, because this man, too, is a son of Abraham."

—Luke 19:5–9 NIV

WHY IS IT IMPORTANT FOR CHRISTIANS TO GIVE OTHERS A SECOND CHANCE?

_____

_____

Think back to a time when you were given a second chance. How do you feel about God giving second chances?

_____

_____

_____

_____

_____

_____

_____

_____

_____

_____

_____

_____

_____

_____

_____

_____

> Be kind and compassionate to one another, forgiving each other, just as in Christ God forgave you.
>
> —Ephesians 4:32 NIV

FORGIVENESS
BRINGS FREEDOM

by Mark Hodge

We all have an image of what the perfect marriage looks like. While most of us don't have that picture-book relationship, we work, with God's guidance, to make our marriages as strong as possible by investing time, energy, and prayer.

When a relationship crumbles, however, whether over time or overnight, it leaves a deep chasm of destruction. Faith is replaced by doubt and cynicism. Self-confidence erodes. Motivation and passion take the nearest exit. Anyone who has experienced the pain of divorce can testify to this truth.

When children are involved, the stakes are even higher. The children of divorce are literally caught in the middle, pulled in multiple directions by well-meaning, concerned parents with different agendas. Sitting across the negotiating table from the one who used to be a trusted partner in life is challenging enough, but trying to negotiate the activities and needs of a child across a fresh line of distrust can be downright impossible, even in the best of circumstances.

As divorced parents struggle with their own turmoil, they are challenged to maintain order and peace for the sake of the children. The routine of parental visits and responsibilities sometimes brings relief, but the hurt of the broken relationship endures long after the final decree signals that the marriage is legally over. There is cruel torment in every encounter and the growing realization that divorce is never really final. Its effects reach across a lifetime.

As time passes, a wall of justification begins to go up. "I am the one who was hurt. Why should I suffer?" Repeated accusations only temporarily gratify the desire to be right. The former couple becomes fixated on making the other person see the error of his or her ways. In the process, they feed their own bitterness and self-destruction.

I wish these were the astute observations of a pastor serving those who have been wounded by divorce, but in reality they represent a firsthand report from the frontlines. I, too, have lived with the aftermath of divorce, and my heart was left longing for peace.

Several years after I was divorced and remarried, I still found myself chained to pain and pride issues. I comforted myself by saying that my turmoil was only natural given what I had been through. I rationalized that time would heal the broken communication. But by refusing to forgive, I was choosing to stay bogged down in the past and provided no grounds to be forgiven for my own wrongdoing. God is very clear in His instructions about this: "For if you forgive men when they sin against you, your heavenly Father will also forgive you" (Matthew 6:14 NIV).

Clearly, I needed to forgive my ex-wife, but I felt God was calling me to do so by writing a letter to her. It took several days for me to compose the letter, and as I wrote, I imagined all the different ways she might respond to it. But when I wrote the final words and sealed it for mailing, something unexpected happened. By confessing my anger, surrendering my pride, and asking for forgiveness, I began to find the elusive peace and healing I was longing for: "A man is a slave to whatever has mastered him" (2 Peter 2:19b NIV). Anger and a lack of forgiveness had enslaved me.

Writing the letter didn't change things overnight. One act of forgiveness did not instantly fix the strained communication between two divorced parents. And it didn't erase the lasting consequences of a broken relationship. But through forgiveness, I found much-needed freedom and peace. You can too.

SCRIPTURE
TO REMEMBER

Therefore, as God's chosen people, holy and dearly loved, clothe yourselves with compassion, kindness, humility, gentleness and patience. Bear with each other and forgive whatever grievances you may have against one another. Forgive as the Lord forgave you.

—Colossians 3:12–13 NIV

QUOTE, UNQUOTE

Forgiveness is unlocking the door to set someone free and realizing you were the prisoner!

—Max Lucado

Are you feeling bitterness toward someone? What would it take to gain your freedom? What benefits would you receive, spiritually and emotionally, if you were to forgive?

TODAY'S PRAYER

Lord, thank You for the freedom that comes from forgiveness. Please show me where I have let my pride enslave me in bitterness or anger toward others. Direct me to the people to whom I need to extend forgiveness and help me to ask humbly for their forgiveness. Please help me demonstrate Your grace in all my relationships.

In Jesus' name, amen.

Then Joseph kissed each of his brothers and wept over them, and after that they began talking freely with him.

—Genesis 45:15 NLT

OH, BROTHER

by Greg Kenerly

Brothers—as you know if you are one or have one—always have stories to tell. While some of your tales may be filled with fun and laughter, others might be filled with anger and sadness. I have an older brother who is bigger than me and could usually take me down in the wrestling matches we had when we were young. Those aren't my fun stories, that's for sure.

Occasionally, he would do something to make me really angry. And when I got angry, I became a different person—kind of like the Incredible Hulk (at least in my mind)! I remember chasing my brother around the yard with a rake on one occasion. Another time, he made me so mad I hit him with a homemade pair of nun chucks, which nearly broke his arm. (Good thing I was a faster runner than he was!) I also remember the time he dragged me around the house by my clip-on suspenders. One of the clips came loose and hit me under the eye. I had to get stitches, and I have the scar to prove it. Can you feel the love?

If you aren't familiar with the story of Joseph in the Old Testament (and even if you are), take a few minutes today to read Genesis 37–45. Joseph's brothers did things that were a lot worse than anything my brother ever did to me. In all fairness to his older brothers, Joseph was probably pretty annoying. If you have a younger brother (or are one), see if this sounds familiar: tattling on his brothers' bad behavior, being daddy's "favorite," bragging about the dreams he had where all his brothers would bow down to him (*every* little brother's dream). All extremely irritating little-brother behaviors.

In Joseph's case, however, his brothers' response was severe. They wanted to have Joseph killed. They initiated a plan, but God had something different in mind. The Bible says Joseph's brothers changed their minds and sold him to a band of traders. They figured the results would be the same—they would be rid of Joseph without having to deal with all the guilt!

Joseph's life from that point on took a number of wild turns—most of them bad. He was subjected to slavery, a false accusation of attempted rape, and prison time. His hopes often were lifted only to be crushed. All in all, Joseph felt like a forgotten man. I'd be hard pressed to find a person who had more reason to hold a grudge than Joseph. It wasn't just something he conjured up in his mind; his brothers had truly wronged him.

TAKE A STAND

The story of Joseph and his brothers is one of the most compelling in the Bible. No matter how many times you've read it, God can teach you valuable lessons from Joseph's trials. Take some time to read about his life in Genesis 37–45.

Often, it seems that family members are the most difficult to forgive. Perhaps, the pain they inflict can be so much deeper because the emotional bonds are so much stronger. If your family situation isn't ideal, you may be wondering where God is in your pain and suffering. As in Joseph's case, God has a plan. He always does.

Joseph endured a great deal of pain and suffering because of his brothers' actions. And just like me, Joseph probably had the scars to prove it. Their actions literally caused him years of misery. And yet, when we read to the end of the story, we see the underpinnings of God's plan. Joseph forgave them, loved them, and literally saved their lives.

Like I've always said, there's nothing like brotherly love!

SCRIPTURE
TO REMEMBER

But Joseph said to them, "Don't be afraid. Am I in the place of God? You intended to harm me, but God intended it for good to accomplish what is now being done, the saving of many lives. So then, don't be afraid. I will provide for you and your children." And he reassured them and spoke kindly to them.

—Genesis 50:19–21 NIV

QUESTION

?

OF THE DAY

DO YOU HAVE A STRAINED RELATIONSHIP WITH A CLOSE FRIEND OR FAMILY MEMBER? CAN TODAY BE THE DAY YOU PUT IT BEHIND YOU BY PRAYING AND REACHING OUT WITH GRACE AND FORGIVENESS?

_____

_____

If you have a strained relationship (family member or friend), take time to write out what you would like to say to that person. If your relationships are all healthy, take time to thank God!

> *And God is able to make all grace abound to you, so that in all things at all times, having all that you need, you will abound in every good work.*
>
> —2 Corinthians 9:8 NIV

QUALIFIED BY GRACE

by Becky Moore

I had the privilege of attending a small group Bible study with a young woman named Liz. Immediately, I recognized she had spiritual depth and sensitivity. I learned that at an early age, she felt God calling her to life on the mission field. But life, sometimes, gets in the way of the calling, and now Liz is married with two kids. While her life stage precluded her from heading overseas to minister, her yearning remained.

At church, she participated in a small group Bible study on God's love and her stirring became stronger. By the end of the study, Liz felt compelled to serve others by volunteering her time to help with office work at a local homeless and prison ministry, Compassion in the Streets. While the ministry's leader, Pastor Howard, appreciated Liz's offer, he challenged her to instead become part of the weekly Bible study his ministry ran at the nearby women's jail.

Not long after she started serving at the jail, Liz was asked to lead the study. Filled with both fear and excitement, she rose to the challenge.

Immediately afterward, she knew that God had just placed her on a mission field. Her earlier call to missions was rekindled and refreshed. From that day, Liz became the Bible study leader for the Women's Jail East in Memphis—her mission field.

Of course, it wasn't always easy. Liz struggled with feelings of inadequacy—what did she have to offer, and could she even relate to these women? One morning, one of Liz's worst fears came true. An inmate looked her in the eyes and asked, "Did you grow up in a nice house with parents who loved you?" Liz responded, "Yes, I did." The inmate replied, "Then who are you to come here and tell us anything?"

Liz knew that God had called her and then empowered her for this ministry. She boldly replied, "I have asked myself and God that same question. My only answer is that I was a sinner and needed to be saved by grace—just like you." Liz's need for God's grace authenticated her ministry—it qualified her for the job God had called her to do.

We are drawn to Christ's forgiveness at the Cross for any number of reasons. While the consequences of our sins may vary greatly, it truly doesn't matter what kind of background we have; we are all sinners in need of God's grace. Despite growing up in the church, one day I found myself broken and humbled in God's presence because of my mediocrity. Being forgiven and set free from prostitution, pride, murder, lying, drunkenness, gossip, bitterness, anger, mediocrity—whatever our sins might be—isn't the issue; that those sins have been covered by Christ's

TAKE A STAND

Ask God to help you see people in need through His eyes and to show you specific ways in which you can serve them. Then, go serve. You will be making a difference as God impacts the people you're serving—and you!

forgiveness is. God doesn't offer less grace for sin that seems less serious by our standards. Sin is sin and that common denominator brings us all to the foot of the Cross where God's grace is enough to cover it all!

In 2 Corinthians 5:17 we read: "Therefore, if anyone is in Christ, he is a new creation; the old has gone, the new has come!" (NIV). Thankfully, because of God's grace, we can all start over as new creations, no matter where we are. Liz continues to serve and minister at the jail, and she often says, "It is the highlight of my week!"

We never know where our mission fields will be. We do know, however, that through God's grace, we can make an impact wherever He places us.

SCRIPTURE
TO REMEMBER

May the God of peace, who through the blood of the eternal covenant brought back from the dead our Lord Jesus, that great Shepherd of the sheep, equip you with everything good for doing his will, and may he work in us what is pleasing to him, through Jesus Christ, to whom be glory for ever and ever. Amen.

—Hebrews 13:20–21 NIV

QUOTE, UNQUOTE

If I have no love for others, no desire to serve others ... I should question whether Christ is really in my life.

—Rick Warren

Your worst days are never so bad that you are beyond the reach of God's grace. And your best days are never so good that you are beyond the need of God's grace.

—Jerry Bridges

Has God called you to do something for Him, but you have been procrastinating? Why? What can you do to get back in action?

> *Be kind to one another, tender-hearted, forgiving each other, just as God in Christ also has forgiven you.*
>
> —Ephesians 4:32 NASB

A GRACE
GAP

by Thom McAdory

Grace is something I'm always ready to read about or talk about. It's a fascinating topic and the stories that come from grace-giving are always compelling. However, even after focusing on it, there are times when I'm not so willing to extend grace to others. That's too bad because when I make that choice, I miss wonderful opportunities to live out grace. I always regret that choice afterward because I feel like I have let everyone down: the person to whom I chose not to give grace; myself for failing in the moment; and, most importantly, God who trusted me with a task I didn't accomplish.

The Bible says that love is kind. Since grace flows out of love, grace looks for ways to be kind. In fact, kindness is one of the ways that grace is given away. Generally speaking, I view myself as a kind person. I open doors for folks. I try to let others go first in the food line—unless I'm really hungry. I'm respectful of others and their feelings. I even try to be understanding when they don't do exactly what I wish they would do.

I have to admit, though, that when I get in my car, all bets are off. The car that turns without using its signal; the pickup truck pulling out in front of me; the semi going ten miles an hour below the speed limit or fifteen above it—these are all problems for me. All it takes is one trip in traffic for me to realize just how unkind I can be. I think the residue that gathers on the inside of my windshield might actually come from my dark thoughts aimed at other drivers.

Strangely, I've noticed a glaring grace gap in my life. I try to appear kind, but my thoughts aren't always kind. Would I rather appear kind and talk about grace in glorious terms, or do I actually want to be kind and offer true grace? In times when I am being less than kind, I wish I was more like my mom—actually I wish I was more like the Jesus she knew and loved.

My mother was the kindest person I have ever known. Mom had a quick mind, she was an avid reader, and she was highly perceptive. She was also hearing impaired. Since our family obviously knew about her lack of hearing, we were able to deal with it easily. But it was a different situation when she came into contact with people who didn't know her. Rude glances and unkind comments were not uncommon. People can be downright mean. →

CHECK LIST

Here are three women in the Bible who are known for having good character—no grace gap for them!

- [ ] Mary, mother of Jesus: "In a loud voice she exclaimed: 'Blessed are you among women, and blessed is the child you will bear!'" (Luke 1:42 NIV).

- [ ] Ruth: "All my fellow townsmen know that you are a woman of noble character" (Ruth 3:11 NIV).

- [ ] Proverbs 31 Woman: "Her children arise and call her blessed; her husband also, and he praises her" (Proverbs 31:28 NIV).

As her son, there were times when I wanted to step up and defend her and return the unkindness that was given to her. But my mom would have none of that; she expected me to respond in kindness. Of course, Mom could also have taken the option to appear kind in public and then complain in private. But that never happened. Mom got it. She knew Christ, she knew that Christ is love, and she knew that grace flows out of love. She was kind in public and kind in private. With her, there was no gap because Jesus was her model.

We could paraphrase Ephesians 4:32 to read, "be kind to one another … as God in Christ has been kind to you." However we look at it, *in Christ* is the key to the verse—and the key to eliminating the grace gap in our lives.

SCRIPTURE
TO REMEMBER

Therefore, my dear friends, as you have always obeyed—not only in my presence, but now much more in my absence—continue to work out your salvation with fear and trembling, for it is God who works in you to will and to act according to his good purpose. Do everything without grumbling or arguing, so that you may become blameless and pure.

—Philippians 2:12–15a NIV

QUOTE, UNQUOTE

Character in a saint means the disposition of Jesus Christ persistently manifested.

—Oswald Chambers

What is your most glaring grace gap? How can you and God team up to overcome it?

USING THE GIFTS
GOD HAS GIVEN YOU

by Lynn Holmes

St. Jude Children's Research Hospital is a Memphis neighbor of ours. The hospital is well known across the nation for their amazing work on behalf of kids. Members of our congregation are employed and minister there. One of them told me the story about a pair of brothers we will call Matt and Michael Wilson.

Four-year-old Michael was diagnosed with cancer just before Christmas and arrived at St. Jude's soon afterward. Christmas was a difficult time, but the Wilsons tried their best to maintain a sense of normalcy for the season. Among the parents' concerns: how nine-year-old Matt would adjust to the new "normal," which included both his parents heading eight hours away to Memphis with Michael, while he stayed with friends and family at home. Would Matt be lost in the shuffle as everyone's focus turned to Michael? The Wilsons were hopeful the brand-new gaming system Matt received for Christmas would help ease the pain of separation.

After putting Michael and Mom on a plane, Dad went back home to say goodbye to Matt before beginning his drive to Memphis.

Matt asked his dad to wait a minute before leaving. He then went into the house, unplugged his new system, and put it carefully in the backseat of the car.

"Dad," he said, "Michael is going to need this more than I am. Could you please make sure to set it up for him when you get to the hospital?"

Matt gave what was most valuable to him without *reluctance* and in that gift, he offered grace to his younger brother, who needed something to take his mind off the struggle he was enduring.

When Matt made his first visit to see Michael in the hospital a few weeks later, he was able to play electronic baseball with his brother. My friend was touched by their companionship and blown away when he heard the whole story from the boys' dad.

"After we learned about Michael, Matt kept asking, 'What can I do for him?' We told him to pray about it and after he did so, Matt handed us the game system. He told us, *'This is what God told me I should do.'* There was not a shred of doubt or question about his decision."

We read in 1 Peter 4:10 that the Holy Spirit has given us a variety of spiritual gifts. I doubt that we would ever consider an electronic game system as a spiritual gift, but the compassion and grace behind the offering certainly is.

In our society of automatic garage door openers, privacy fences, security systems, and caller IDs, it is easy to lose touch with our neighbors. Yet, if we were to take the time to know them, we might notice their hurts, their loneliness, their concerns, their dilemmas. The Bible teaches us that everything we *have* and everything we *are* is a gift from God. And this verse reminds us that we are to use whatever gifts we have to serve others. In doing so, we become a face of grace to those around us.

All of us who have experienced the love of God, who understand the pain of failure and the healing salve of encouragement—*all* of us have something to offer others! If grace is simply reflecting the character of Christ, then encouragement, acceptance, acts of kindness, and even sharing an electronic gaming system are worshipful acts of grace.

SCRIPTURE
TO REMEMBER

"'For I was hungry and you gave me something to eat, I was thirsty and you gave me something to drink, I was a stranger and you invited me in, I needed clothes and you clothed me, I was sick and you looked after me, I was in prison and you came to visit me.' Then the righteous will answer him, 'Lord, when did we see you hungry and feed you, or thirsty and give you something to drink? When did we see you a stranger and invite you in, or needing clothes and clothe you? When did we see you sick or in prison and go to visit you?' The King will reply, 'I tell you the truth, whatever you did for one of the least of these brothers of mine, you did for me.'"

—Matthew 25:35–40 NIV

de•fin•ing moment

SPIRITUAL GIFTS: "A SPECIAL DIVINE EMPOWERMENT BESTOWED ON EACH BELIEVER BY THE HOLY SPIRIT TO ACCOMPLISH A GIVEN MINISTRY ACCORDING TO GOD'S GRACE AND DISCERNMENT AND TO BE USED WITHIN THE CONTEXT OF THE BODY OF CHRIST."

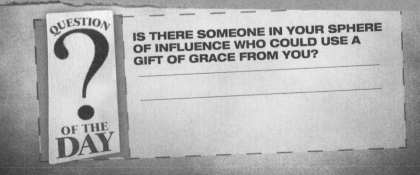

QUESTION ? OF THE DAY

IS THERE SOMEONE IN YOUR SPHERE OF INFLUENCE WHO COULD USE A GIFT OF GRACE FROM YOU?

What talents and abilities do you have that could be used to reflect the character of Christ into someone's life? What are some ways you could put these abilities into action?

_____

_____

_____

_____

_____

_____

_____

_____

_____

_____

_____

_____

_____

_____

_____

At once he began to preach in the synagogues that Jesus is the Son of God.

—Acts 9:20 NIV

FADING FRIENDSHIPS

by Daniel Medders

I have a friend who is tremendously talented and incredibly creative. He is neither of these, however, when it comes to his friendships. Over the years that we've been friends, many of his other friendships have come and gone. While he has the uncanny ability to befriend people, these friendships don't seem to last long term. That has always intrigued me … and saddened me, as well.

When we look at the life of the Apostle Paul, we can gain insights into what is required to maintain the important relationships we have with family, neighbors, and friends. When we first meet Paul, he is known by his original name, Saul, and he sees the recently crucified Christ as a threat to his religion and his way of life. Christ and His followers were, in Saul's eyes, a disgrace to the Jewish faith and an evil that needed to be purged. So Saul began to lead tyrannical raids designed to persecute those who followed Jesus.

Saul's misplaced passion is first noted in Acts 8 as he stands watching the stoning of Stephen and "giving approval to his death." As we continue to read about him in Acts 9, we find Saul "still breathing out murderous threats." A powerful man, Saul had the authority to enter the temple to remove anyone considered to be a follower of Jesus. Saul was convinced that these Christians were dangerous, and he was willing to do whatever it took to eradicate them.

One day, on his way to Damascus, Saul encountered God in an incredible way. He appeared in the form of a bright, blinding light. From that point on, the newly named Paul—a man once consumed by a mission to rid the world of Christians—was convicted of his wrongdoing and immediately began to preach the Gospel of Christ.

Like Saul, my friend seems to dismiss people due to their past mistakes. When someone lets him down or disappoints him, he quickly removes that person from his list of trustworthy people. Depending on the impact of the mistake, he might even choose to remove him or her completely from his life. One thing I've noticed about people: They will let us down. It may not always be intentional, but it is a reality. It's no wonder my friend is living a life with few lasting friendships.

TAKE A STAND

Can you think of someone who was once important in your life but you have now written off? Pray about extending grace to that person and re-establishing the friendship.

Going back to Saul, it's obvious that God desired to have a relationship with him, despite the fact Saul was doing things that God did not condone. Yet, no matter how much harm, hate, and malice Saul had exhibited toward Christians, God still worked to reach Saul, so that He could use the new believer to reach others.

God is obviously willing to give us second (and third and fourth and fifth) chances. Shouldn't we be willing to give the people in our lives at least a second chance? One thing God never does is write anyone off—not Saul, not me, not you. We've all been wronged. And we've all wronged others, and we've all wronged God. We know that God forgives us. The question is: Are we willing to forgive others?

SCRIPTURE
TO REMEMBER

As [Saul] neared Damascus on his journey, suddenly a light from heaven flashed around him. He fell to the ground and heard a voice say to him, "Saul, why do you persecute me?" "Who are you, Lord?" Saul asked. "I am Jesus, whom you are persecuting," he replied.

—Acts 9:3–5 NIV

TODAY'S PRAYER

Lord, You are the God of second chances. Thank You for all the times You have been there for me when I haven't deserved it. Please soften my heart so I can see the people You've put in my life as You see them—precious and worthy of multiple second chances. Help me re-establish my broken friendship by extending Your grace to my former friend. I trust You for the outcome and thank You for the opportunity, in Jesus' name. Amen.

What went wrong in the friendship you feel God wants you to re-establish? What will you need to say to offer grace? Write out your thoughts in preparation.

GRACE IS A PLATE
OF WARM COOKIES

by Greg Nash

When we became members of our church, Miss Anne was the first person to welcome my family. A widow, Anne had many needs and concerns of her own, but she always made it a priority to reach out and care for others, especially when it came to the delivery of her warm, home-baked cookies.

While Miss Anne made us feel special, it was nothing extraordinary for her; it was her way of sharing God's love, both at church and in her neighborhood. She often visited a neighbor named Robert and his family, taking them her delicious cookies. During each visit, Miss Anne would also invite them to go to church with her, but they consistently responded with a polite, but firm, "No."

Time passed, and Miss Anne continued to show the love of Christ and offer His grace to the family. Not once in more than twenty-five years, however, did they visit her church. Then Robert was diagnosed with cancer, and his wife soon left him to battle the disease—and raise their two teenage children—alone. Miss Anne asked our pastor to visit

Robert in the hospital, and as the pastor prayed for him during that visit, Robert accepted God's saving grace.

In the months that followed, Robert's health began to improve, and he started attending our church with Miss Anne. During this time, though, Miss Anne's health began to decline, and she was no longer able to drive. So, in a God-ordained twist of grace, Robert began bringing Miss Anne to church with him every Sunday! He also became actively involved with our church's jail ministry, which allowed him to share his testimony with the inmates. God had done a mighty work in his life, and Robert wanted everyone to know about it.

Sadly, a few months later, Robert's cancer returned with a vengeance and within weeks, he lost his battle. At his funeral, story after story after story was shared about how Robert's life—and God's grace—had impacted others. As I looked at frail Miss Anne sitting in the pew, I couldn't help but marvel at how God's grace and love, when offered faithfully and consistently, always pays dividends. Grace can be as simple and heartfelt as a plate of warm, fresh-baked cookies, and that same grace can change lives for eternity and build the Kingdom of God in mighty ways!

We are called to be God's grace through loving , caring for, and reaching out to people in their times of need. God's grace is in the faithful sharing of His love, even when that love is not ➤

CHECK LIST

Maybe baking cookies isn't your forte. Here are three simple ways you can serve people you know with God's love:

☐ Offer to watch a neighbor's house (and pet) while they travel.

☐ Share from the abundance of your garden's harvest.

☐ Provide childcare for a single mom in your neighborhood.

received immediately. It is in these simple offerings of grace that God's love is shown and His Kingdom is built. There are people all around us who are lonely, hurting, and dying. Some of these people might never acknowledge this, but they need to be loved. We all need to be loved. And there is no love more perfect than God's love for us through Christ.

What better way to introduce people to God's love than by sharing it? As the opportunity affords itself (and it will!), remember to tell others that it is Christ's love that compels us to give, care, and share. Sometimes, they will eagerly receive that message. Other times, it might take a simple act of kindness to lead them to God's grace and forgiveness—something like a plate of warm cookies.

SCRIPTURE
TO REMEMBER

[God] has saved us and called us to a holy life—not because of anything we have done but because of his own purpose and grace. This grace was given us in Christ Jesus before the beginning of time, but it has now been revealed through the appearing of our Savior, Christ Jesus, who has destroyed death and has brought life and immortality to light through the gospel.

—2 Timothy 1:9–10 NIV

" QUOTE, UNQUOTE "

Grace is the good pleasure of God that inclines Him to bestow benefits upon the undeserving. ... Its use to us sinful men is to save us and make us sit together in heavenly places to demonstrate to the ages the exceeding riches of God's kindness to us in Christ Jesus.

—A. W. Tozer

Who are the people who shared God's love and grace with you? Take time to remember and thank God for them.

> "Come to me, all you who are weary and burdened, and I will give you rest. Take my yoke upon you and learn from me, for I am gentle and humble in heart, and you will find rest for your souls. For my yoke is easy and my burden is light."
>
> —Matthew 11:28–30 NIV

THE IRON
SKILLET

by Greg Kenerly

Each spring, some of the men from our church go backpacking on the Appalachian Trail. While none of us are true "mountain men," a few have hiked it enough times to know how to prepare. Others, though, have never spent a night in the woods, which is why we always hold an informational meeting ahead of time to let them know what to expect and what to bring.

Packing light is essential. We remind them that we must carry everything we bring on our backs—food, water, clothing, tents, and everything else. The less they bring, the lighter their pack … and ten miles into the trail, a lighter pack is much nicer than a heavier one. A few pounds make a big difference on the trail.

That's why I make it a point to eat a lot of noodles and oatmeal. They are light and all you have to do is add hot water. On my friend Stephen's first hike with us, he brought a wide variety of food, *plus* a large iron skillet to cook it in. So while we were eating noodles and oatmeal, he ate things like lasagna, and ham and cheese omelets. We didn't like Stephen very much at meal times. But Stephen paid a steep price. An iron skillet gets heavy when you carry it with you every step you take. That extra weight began to slow him down, and he began to lag behind the rest of the group. Of course, we "noodles and oatmeal" guys didn't have much sympathy. At one point, Stephen was so far behind us that we couldn't see him. Eventually, he caught up and stayed with us the rest of the way. While he never admitted it, I'm guessing that somewhere in those mountains of North Georgia, an iron skillet is rusting away.

Our walk through life is sometimes like that. As a pastor, I've unfortunately seen too many people choose to hold on to their "iron skillets." Issues like grudges and unforgiveness slow them down. We cannot keep those heavy items in our packs and expect to make it to the end. The grace card we see offered in the movie of the same name says in part: "I will ask your forgiveness and grant you the same."

Have you been holding on to a hurt or grudge for a long time? Maybe it's time to unload that iron skillet by granting forgiveness—even if the person you're forgiving hasn't asked for it.

Write your hurt down on a piece of paper. Pray about it and give it to God. Then tear the paper into tiny pieces and throw it away. Make today the day you begin packing the right way for your journey—light and unencumbered.

QUESTION ? OF THE DAY

HEBREWS 12:1 SAYS THAT WE MUST "STRIP OFF EVERY WEIGHT THAT SLOWS US DOWN" (NLT) IN OUR WALK WITH GOD. CHRIST SAYS TO TRADE YOKES WITH HIM IN MATTHEW 11. WHAT HEAVY BURDENS DO YOU NEED TO THROW OFF AND GIVE TO JESUS?

_____

_____

QUOTE, UNQUOTE

A chip on the shoulder is too heavy a piece of baggage to carry through life.

—John Hancock

What trail does God have you on these days? What are you learning about yourself and about Him as you go along your way?

TODAY'S PRAYER

Dear Lord, please forgive me for any grudge that I'm currently holding. Help me to remember that by carrying these I only hurt myself. Help me to become more forgiving, knowing that You are always willing to forgive me. Thanks for helping me toss away my iron skillets and take on the yoke You give me. In Christ's name, amen.

Jesus said to him, "I tell you the truth, today you will be with me in paradise."

—Luke 23:43 NCV

GRACE IN
LINGERING

by Becky Moore

While studying the Book of John in a community Bible study, God gave me fresh insights on a passage of Scripture that I had been familiar with for years. I understood that Jesus Christ's death on the Cross was the ultimate example of grace in the Bible. Pure and sinless, He laid down His life and endured extreme suffering so that we could experience forgiveness and freedom from the bondage of sin. Because Jesus was God in flesh, He did not have to suffer; He had the power to return to His throne and the comforts of heaven. What I hadn't realized was that He could have died the moment the Cross was raised and still fulfilled His purpose: to be the sacrifice for the sin of mankind.

God showed me that He willingly and purposefully lingered. That may seem like a strange word choice … until you consider that the word linger means "to remain, to hang around, to delay leaving." Jesus literally lingered in His suffering on the Cross for the sake of those around Him that day.

Mary, His mother, was present at the foot of the Cross, and Jesus thoughtfully cared for her during His final moments on earth. In John 19:26–27 we read: "When Jesus saw his mother there, and the disciple whom he loved standing nearby, he said to his mother, "Dear woman, here is your son," and to the disciple, "Here is your mother." From that time on, this disciple took her into his home" (NIV).

Jesus' love for both John and Mary was evident in His tender words as He passed the responsibility of Mary's care to His beloved friend John. Jesus' grace was displayed as He lingered for the sake of His mother's future.

Three crosses are common when we picture Christ's crucifixion scene. It reminds us that two other men were crucified that day, as well. We learn in Matthew 27:44 and Mark 15:32 that these men were robbers who heaped insults on Jesus from the earliest stages of His crucifixion. Scripture is unclear as to what happened to change one of the robber's attitudes, but in Luke 23:39–43 we read:

One of the criminals who hung there hurled insults at him: "Aren't you the Christ? Save yourself and us!" But the other criminal rebuked him. "Don't you fear God," he said, "since you are under the same sentence? We are punished justly, for we are getting what our deeds deserve. But this man has done nothing wrong." Then he said, "Jesus, remember me when you come into your kingdom." Jesus answered him, "I tell you the truth, today you will be with me in paradise" (NIV).

Lingering in death for your mother and a dear friend is one thing, but to suffer longer than what is required for a criminal who insults you? Now that's a display of grace. Jesus knew this robber needed salvation, and He was willing to wait for Him to acknowledge his need. Jesus' grace was once again demonstrated as He lingered for the salvation of a common criminal.

I have learned so much from Christ's example of lingering. Unfortunately, for me—and most of the people I know—busyness is a way of life, and it's the enemy of lingering. It causes us to miss out on wonderful opportunities to show grace to others. Yet Jesus took time for others, even during extreme pain and suffering.

Following Christ's example and slowing down will give us the time we need to really see those around us who need us to linger for them and give them God's grace. Will you linger today?

SCRIPTURE
TO REMEMBER

The Lord is not slow in keeping his promise, as some understand slowness. He is patient with you, not wanting anyone to perish, but everyone to come to repentance.

—2 Peter 3:9 NIV

de•fin•ing moment

LINGER: "TO BE SLOW IN LEAVING, ESPECIALLY OUT OF RELUCTANCE." ON EARTH, JESUS WAS RELUCTANT TO LEAVE. IN HEAVEN, JESUS LINGERS SO THAT EVERYONE HAS AN OPPORTUNITY TO COME TO HIM FOR FORGIVENESS AND GRACE.

TODAY'S PRAYER

Dear Lord, thank You for lingering on the Cross to show Your incredible love for all—those who knew You best and those just meeting You. Thank You for lingering in heaven so that the people You love, and the people I love, will continue to have an opportunity to know You. Help me to be generous in my willingness to linger and bold in sharing Your grace with the people You've put in my world. I trust You for the outcome.

In Jesus' name, amen.

What does lingering for a friend mean to you? How can you find time in your schedule for lingering?

_____
_____
_____
_____
_____
_____
_____
_____
_____
_____
_____
_____
_____
_____
_____
_____
_____
_____
_____
_____
_____
_____
_____

> *"His father saw him and was filled with compassion for him; he ran to his son, threw his arms around him and kissed him."*
>
> —Luke 15:20b NIV

COMPELLED
TO GRACE

by Thom McAdory

The story of the prodigal son has been preached, taught, and studied throughout the centuries. And the beauty of the story is that there is always something new to discover. But one thing that's consistent is this: The two sons, each in their own selfishness, are a stark contrast to their father's love and grace.

I love the image of the father looking day after day to see if his younger son—the one who had taken his inheritance and disappeared—might be heading home. He'll watch as long as it takes. All he wants is for his son to come home again.

As a parent, I have come to understand this parable with clarity—perhaps, more than I could ever have wanted to. The heart-wrenching desire to see your offspring come to know God and serve Him consumes an inordinate amount of time, emotion, and prayer. I imagine the father of this prodigal walking out to the road as often as he can, stretching his vision to the horizon, hoping to catch a glimpse of the son he has lost. His example has helped me learn that I need to keep a grace-filled heart toward those who have gone off to their own far country.

The spiritual implications from this parable are enormous. The prodigal, in our eyes, didn't deserve the kind of grace he received in great measure, grace offered even before he returned home. His father's hope and forgiveness reached across the distance to touch a hard-hearted son. Think of the prayers the father must have prayed, the times he despaired at not seeing them answered. And then, there must have been the unsettling thoughts that his son might be gone forever.

Fortunately, for the prodigal's father, there was a happy outcome. One day, as he looked off in the distance, he saw his son coming! He lifted up his dignified robes and, with no regard for how it looked, he ran as fast as he could to greet his long-lost boy.

The obvious take-away from this story is that God always gives grace to His prodigals—us. But I believe there is something else here too: what happens when we withhold grace. The prodigal's older brother turns a cold shoulder to his returning brother and disrespects his father. He goes through his days waiting for the time when he will inherit his father's wealth, without a thought of sharing it with anyone. And when his brother—"this son of yours"—returns home, he wants nothing to do with the celebration of grace. Hard to believe this loving father raised these two sons!

This story reminds me that if the Father, by His Spirit, lives in me, I should be actively seeking ways to extend grace to prodigals—including those who seem the least worthy of grace. Extending grace does not cost me anything. It's a way I can freely give of my inheritance on a daily basis. Like the father in the story, I just need to constantly be on the lookout for my opportunities.

SCRIPTURE
TO REMEMBER

"Suppose one of you has a hundred sheep and loses one of them. Does he not leave the ninety-nine in the open country and go after the lost sheep until he finds it? And when he finds it, he joyfully puts it on his shoulders and goes home. Then he calls his friends and neighbors together and says, 'Rejoice with me; I have found my lost sheep.' I tell you that in the same way there will be more rejoicing in heaven over one sinner who repents than over ninety-nine righteous persons who do not need to repent."

—Luke 15:4–7 NIV

de•fin•ing moment

PRODIGAL: "A PERSON WHO SPENDS (OR HAS SPENT) HIS OR HER MONEY WITH WASTEFUL EXTRAVAGANCE."

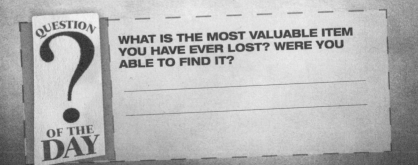

QUESTION ? OF THE DAY

WHAT IS THE MOST VALUABLE ITEM YOU HAVE EVER LOST? WERE YOU ABLE TO FIND IT?

The father longed for the return of his son. What is your heart's greatest longing these days?

> "Be merciful, just as your Father is merciful. Do not judge, and you will not be judged. Do not condemn, and you will not be condemned. Forgive, and you will be forgiven."
>
> —Luke 6:36–37 NIV

MIGHTIER
THAN THE FIST

by Greg Kenerly

One of the highlights of my role as a youth pastor is going to summer camp—well, except for all that sweating and those gnats! But beyond that, camp is a great time to hang out and build relationships with students.

One church I served at was predominantly Caucasian, but our student ministry also included a number of Jamaican- and African-American students. We saw one another as friends—not black friends and white friends—just friends, and it was a beautiful thing. Unfortunately, not everyone saw things the way we did.

William, an African-American student from our group, was the only non-white teen at a summer camp of about two hundred fifty area students. William had been part of our church for years, and he was one of the most "solid" Christians in our youth ministry. He was a real leader with a passion for God. William was fun, handsome, athletic, and everyone who knew him liked him.

The problem arose with kids who didn't *know* him. Like Sam in *The Grace Card*, William was often judged solely by the color of his skin.

As we spent part of a fun evening in a town near the camp, several students from the local community joined our group. Though I'd noticed the teens earlier, I was unaware that they had followed us back to the campground.

I was standing by the snack shack when William came bursting through the side door shouting, "They're trying to get me; they're trying to get me!" He was obviously extremely frightened. William said that when he was heading to the snack shop, he saw some guys who seemed to be looking for him. He sensed trouble and ran for the door, but they grabbed him and started beating him. Somehow, William managed to get away from them and run for help.

One of the camp counselors from the area thought he might know who was responsible. He left camp, and we waited for him to bring the police back. Instead, he returned with someone else—the leader of the group of boys who had attacked William.

After the counselor found the boy, he asked him why he and his friends had attacked William. The local teen said it was because they didn't like that William had been talking with white girls and felt they needed to "teach him a lesson." The man told the teen that he either needed to apologize to William or explain what happened to the police. The teen came back to the camp. With several adults standing guard, the teen, instead of apologizing, said to William, "Why don't you just punch me in the face and we'll call it even?"

What happened next left us all speechless. William said, "Instead of me punching you, how 'bout I hug you, tell you I love you, and tell you I wish you could see me for more than the color of my skin." William then wrapped his arms around the confused and speechless attacker.

What an amazing moment! I watched as real hatred was stared down and defeated by the loving and grace-filled words and actions of a high school student named William. He had the opportunity to play the race card; instead, he chose to play the grace card.

de•fin•ing moment

PREJUDICE: "AN ADVERSE JUDGMENT OR OPINION FORMED BEFOREHAND OR WITHOUT KNOWLEDGE OR EXAMINATION OF THE FACTS."

QUOTE, UNQUOTE

Darkness cannot drive out darkness; only light can do that. Hate cannot drive out hate; only love can do that. Hate multiplies hate, violence multiplies violence, and toughness multiplies toughness in a descending spiral of destruction.

—Martin Luther King, Jr.

Who of a different race or ethnicity could you get to know better with a little extra effort? Brainstorm some ideas for reaching out to them in friendship.

_____

_____

_____

_____

_____

_____

_____

_____

_____

TODAY'S PRAYER

Lord, examine my heart and bring to mind any wrong attitudes I have toward people who are different from me. Please forgive me for the times I judge people simply because of how they look or speak. Please help me forge a new friendship with someone who is different from me. And help me remember that You see both them and me with the same eyes. Thank You for loving each of us so much that You gave Your only Son.

In His name I pray. Amen.

BRINGING OUT
THE BEST IN OTHERS

by Lynn Holmes

If you've ever stayed in a hotel, you've heard of Gideon. And, depending on how knowledgeable you were about faith issues growing up, you may have even thought Gideon wrote the Bible. Actually, Gideon is a great character in the Old Testament ... but he didn't start out that way!

Gideon was in the midst of an identity crisis when we meet him. He viewed himself as the runt of his family—and his family came from the smallest tribe of the nation of Israel. Now, that's small. In Chapter 6 of Judges, we read that Gideon was in a winepress, hiding from an opposing army. Clearly this man had self-esteem issues.

So how did God's angel greet Gideon? "The LORD is with you, mighty warrior" (Judges 6:12 NIV). God didn't factor in how Gideon saw himself; no, God's messenger addressed Gideon as he was seen in heaven's eyes. In the story that follows, we learn that God was able to use this warrior in mighty ways.

Gideon is a great example of an important truth: Our Lord is an encourager! He recognizes our potential and sees us not necessarily as we *are*, but as we *could become* through His grace and power. Jesus did this with Peter. When He first met Peter, his name was Simon, which means *small pebble*. But Jesus renamed him *Cephas*, which means *the rock*! (See John 1:42 NIV.)

Yet, when Jesus first called him "the Rock," Peter was anything but. Names that might have been a better fit include "Mr. Impulsive," "Mr. Foot-in-the-Mouth," and the ever-popular, "Mr. Hey Let's Walk on Water and Sink!" But Jesus recognized Peter's potential, not his failures. Our Lord always brings out the best in others; He is in the people-building business.

We all need encouragement, but in this day and age, it seems to be in short supply. We are fully cognizant of our weaknesses and failures, and we fear that's all others see when they look at us. Having someone who believes in us and sees our potential is like a breath of fresh air in a stale world.

The Bible teaches us to consider our neighbors and build up their character. I believe Christianity should be synonymous with kindness. Acts of kindness naturally point people to Christ, and as we grow deeper in our relationship with the people we are building up, we have the opportunity to share God's grace with them. If we are to be a "face of grace" to others, we need to see their potential and encourage them to pursue it. So look for ways to genuinely, sincerely, and regularly encourage others.

Recognizing what people do well and seeing their potential is a gift rarely offered. Fortunately, Jesus Christ always sees the potential in us; as ambassadors of His grace, we need to bring out the best in others, as well.

First 1 Thessalonians 5:11 reminds us to "encourage one another and build each other up" (NIV). When you see people doing something well, recognition and a pat on the back will go a long way. If you keep your eyes open for ways to encourage others, you will become a vessel of grace, and you will reflect the character of Jesus Christ, who is to be a model for us all. Now that's encouraging!

HOMEWORK ASSIGNMENT

Read Judges 6–9 and John 1:35–51. Highlight some of the ways that God sees the possibilities in His people and through His grace enables them to achieve their full potential. What other examples can you find in the Bible that speak of God building up His people?

QUOTE, UNQUOTE

A manager's task is to make the strengths of people effective and their weaknesses irrelevant.

—Peter Drucker

Do you know someone who could use your encouragement? In what ways do they need to be encouraged?

_____

_____

_____

_____

_____

_____

_____

_____

_____

_____

TODAY'S PRAYER

Dear Lord, thank You for being my encourager and thanks for the people You've placed in my life who use their encouraging words to lift me up. Please forgive me for the times I have chosen to tear people down rather than build them up. Help me see the potential of the people in my world, and help me become an encourager in their lives. Thanks for the opportunities You will provide. In Jesus' name, amen.

At this the man's face fell. He went away sad, because he had great wealth.

—Mark 10:22 NIV

WE CAN ONLY
OFFER GRACE

by Daniel Medders

My cell phone rang one Sunday afternoon as I was enjoying a well-prepared rib-eye steak. Assuming it to be nothing but an unwanted distraction from my delicious dinner, I was taken aback when I heard a woman from my church on the other line. Jason, a teenaged member of her family, had just been diagnosed with terminal cancer. I immediately lost all interest in my meal.

Like many other seventeen-year-olds, Jason played sports and enjoyed the outdoors. His friends made up a big component of his life. Like most teens, he felt invincible and assumed he could conquer anything in his path, including this insidious disease. His cancer, however, was unwavering. When I talked with my friend about Jason, she was concerned that he did not have a relationship with Christ. She asked me to visit him in the hospital.

Within an hour, I was in Jason's hospital room. He was lying in bed watching a television program, but I could tell he was visibly shaken. As we began to chat about life, sports, and other topics, it became clear that we had a lot in common. We played the same position in football, we were about the same size, and we enjoyed many of the same hobbies.

We shared some fishing stories and football memories before I turned the conversation in a spiritual direction. I asked Jason about his relationship with God, and he informed me that he had never asked Jesus to be Lord of his life. Knowing that he might be staring eternity in the face, I asked him expectantly if he would like to pray with me to invite Christ into his heart.

I will never forget how this seventeen-year-old, dying of cancer, looked around for a second and responded, "No thanks, I'm fine not knowing God." I was shocked. After we talked for a while longer, he began to withdraw from the conversation. He eventually became reclusive and quiet as he avoided talking to me. Taking that as my cue, I said goodbye to Jason.

When I made it back to my truck, I wept. I had never seen someone so much in need willingly reject the gift of salvation. After our initial connections, I had imagined our faith conversation would end much differently—at the foot of the Cross. I was sure Jason would pray for salvation; I was already thinking ahead to sharing an incredible story with my church in celebration. Instead, I went back to my truck filled with sadness over Jason's rejection of God.

Jason died a few days after I saw him. I'm still tormented by his response, which was not unlike that of the rich young ruler we meet in the Bible. That young man knew in his heart that he wanted to follow Jesus. He just couldn't wrap his mind around the cost of doing so.

I learned a lot from Jason, including *I'm* not able to save anyone. Just because I share the incredible message of the Gospel with someone, doesn't mean that person will accept an invitation to follow Jesus. Not everyone will accept Christ's saving grace. Yet as believers, we need to continue to offer God's grace to everyone we meet. We must remember, however, that the decision to accept His grace is not our responsibility, but theirs. Our responsibility is to live out our faith in front of them and point them toward the grace that God has offered to each and every one of us.

SCRIPTURE
TO REMEMBER

" For God so loved the world that he gave his one and only Son, that whoever believes in him shall not perish but have eternal life. For God did not send his Son into the world to condemn the world, but to save the world through him. Whoever believes in him is not condemned, but whoever does not believe stands condemned already because he has not believed in the name of God's one and only Son.

—John 3:16–18 NIV

de•fin•ing moment

SALVATION: "DELIVERANCE FROM THE POWER AND PENALTY OF SIN; REDEMPTION."

QUOTE, UNQUOTE

Suppose you could gain everything in the whole world, and lost your soul. Was it worth it?

— Billy Graham

Is God calling you to share His grace with someone? What are the barriers that have kept you from following through? Pray and map out your plan to do so.

_____

_____

_____

_____

_____

_____

_____

_____

_____

_____

_____

_____

_____

CAN GOD
TRUST YOU?

by Greg Kenerly

When I was a young man, I became sort-of engaged. How do you do that, you ask? Well, after driving to see my girlfriend eight hundred thirty miles away, we discussed getting married and what that might look like. But at that point, there wasn't a ring, and we hadn't set a wedding date. After our time together, I headed home, thinking of ways I might be able to buy an engagement ring to make my sort-of engagement an official one. It wouldn't be easy since I had only three hundred dollars in the bank—but at least that was a start.

Unfortunately, that long drive home proved to be costly. I was about six hours from home when the "Check Engine" light lit up my dashboard. I found a service station with a mechanic on duty. He took one look and determined that my alternator was about to give out. I decided to hit the road quickly, knowing darkness would soon fall—and a bad alternator would mean no headlights! Somehow, I made it home and drove straight to the auto repair shop where my car literally died as I pulled into the parking lot. I was relieved, though ever so briefly. Two days later when the repairs were complete, my bill was a whopping two hundred seventy-eight dollars! My heart sank as I realized that paying for the car repair would leave me with only twenty-two dollars in my bank account for what I had hoped would be the most amazing engagement ring ever!

I was discouraged by the "fact" that God had let me down. I felt strongly that I needed to have a conversation with Him about all that had happened. I headed into the quiet sanctuary of the church where I worked, and began to really let God have it. I reminded Him that I had been faithful, that I always paid my tithe, and that I was serving Him with my life. I explained that I wasn't obsessed with money; I just wanted to be able to get married and support my wife.

Once I finished stating my case to God, I left the sanctuary and headed outside to get the church's mail. As I glanced through it, I noticed a letter addressed to me. Inside the envelope was a letter from the owner of the auto repair shop that had worked on my car—a man I had never met before. The letter simply said, "I felt like God was telling me I needed to give this back to you." And there, folded up inside the envelope, was the check I had written two days earlier for →

CHECK LIST

Here are three ways God can use you to make a difference in someone's life today:

- [ ] 1) Send a note of thanks to someone who has served you in a meaningful way.

- [ ] 2) Give a grocery store gift card anonymously to a family that is in a difficult financial situation.

- [ ] 3) Visit and encourage the residents in a senior citizens' home.

the repair of my car. While I can't be theologically certain of this, I'm pretty sure God was laughing at me in that moment.

I learned many lessons about my faith through that experience. I also realized that the shop owner probably had, as well. If he had not been obedient, his failure to do what God asked him to do would have profoundly affected both of us. He extended grace to me by an act of kindness. I'm sure he wondered why God was asking him to do such a thing—but God knew exactly what was going on. And that shop owner trusted God.

God knew He could trust the shop owner to be obedient. And because of that shop owner's obedience, I learned that I could trust God completely.

SCRIPTURE
TO REMEMBER

As he was going into a village, ten men who had leprosy met him. They stood at a distance and called out in a loud voice, "Jesus, Master, have pity on us!" When he saw them, he said, "Go, show yourselves to the priests." And as they went, they were cleansed. One of them, when he saw he was healed, came back, praising God in a loud voice. He threw himself at Jesus' feet and thanked him.

—Luke 17:12–16a NIV

TAKE A STAND

While we may not understand why God asks us to do something for someone, we still need to heed His call; after all, He sees the big picture. Is there something God is asking you to do that might not seem logical? Is there someone to whom you could show an act of kindness, extend grace, and give God the credit for it? Do it today and your obedience could make a big difference in someone's life!

Write about a time when you clearly saw God's
hand of provision in your life.

Praise be to the God and Father of our Lord Jesus Christ, who has blessed us in the heavenly realms with every spiritual blessing in Christ … to the praise of His glorious grace, which he has freely given us.

—Ephesians 1:3, 6a NIV

FUNDING
GRACE

by Thom McAdory

In my many years of pastoral ministry, I've known people who seem to operate on reserves of joy. No matter their circumstances, they are joyful. These are the kinds of people we love to be around because they are so encouraging and uplifting. Of course, the opposite is true, as well—there are people who are so negative and hurtful that we feel better when we *don't* interact with them!

In the movie *The Grace Card*, Mac is an angry and hurtful individual. He provides a vivid example of the old maxim, "hurt people hurt people." When Mac is angry, he wounds others—and he's angry most of the time. A deep pain that can never go away has left Mac embittered. Unfortunately, most of us know someone like Mac.

Some people in Mac's situation become frustrated by their own actions and attitudes, and their inability to change their behavior. The truth is, changing this kind of attitude or behavior must come from a source beyond ourselves. Anger management training can't provide the change we need, the kind that offers hope to a heart that has been hardened. Only God's grace can turn us away from our habitual hurtful acts and toward the extension of grace.

So how does that change occur? It is as though a new economy is needed—an exchange must take place. In the economy of grace, funds have to be available in order to give grace away. Yet, I cannot fund the account on my own. We can only truly give grace when we've made a grace-exchange—I must be willing to trade my hurt for God's healing, my anger for His peace, my hurtful acts for His forgiveness, and my self-centeredness for God-centeredness.

When I allow God's Spirit to move in my life, He fills me with grace so I have resources to draw from. The more grace-filled I am, the more naturally I offer grace to others. Grace is free to flow through me to others in the form of prayers, forgiveness, and fellowship. The beauty of this economy is that God willingly continues to fund my account with the blessing of His grace. I then pass that grace on to others, and God refills my account.

It's hard for me to forgive or pray for someone who has hurt me. But when we truly understand what grace offers—forgiveness, goodness, peace—it becomes easier to offer grace to someone else, no matter the circumstances.

Despite our growing understanding of God's grace, there are still times when we feel inadequate for the task of offering grace to others. That is natural. But God has promised the supernatural: "My grace is sufficient for you, for my power is made perfect in

TAKE A STAND

Knowing that God will not ask us to do something He is not first willing to fund in abundance (See Ephesians 1:7–8.), where specifically can you offer His grace today? Will you?

weakness" (2 Corinthians 12:9 NIV). In the economy of grace, God is always looking for the opportunity to add to our grace fund: "And God is able to make all grace abound to you, so that in all things at all times, having all that you need, you will abound in every good work" (2 Corinthians 9:8 NIV).

Like Sam in the movie, those of us who know Christ are called to be His agents of grace. Isn't it good to know that we have the unlimited resources provided by the God of the universe? He is always on our side, as we extend the grace card to the Macs in our world.

de•fin•ing moment

EXCHANGE: "TO GIVE UP SOMETHING FOR SOMETHING ELSE; PART WITH FOR SOME EQUIVALENT; CHANGE FOR ANOTHER."

GRACE EXCHANGE: "TO PART WITH PAIN TO RECEIVE GOD'S JOY; NOTHING EQUIVALENT ABOUT IT!"

" QUOTE, UNQUOTE "

A man can no more take in a supply of grace for the future than he can eat enough today to last him for the next six months. Nor can he inhale sufficient air into his lungs with one breath to sustain life for a week to come. We are permitted to draw upon God's store of grace from day to day as we need it.

—Dwight L. Moody

Remember a time when you fully tapped into God's resources to extend grace to someone. What were the results for that person and for you?

Show proper respect to everyone.

—1 Peter 2:17a NIV

A POLITENESS
REVOLUTION

by Lynn Holmes

As a pastor, I am committed to treating everyone with respect and compassion. Unfortunately, that's a common courtesy that seems to be less common with each passing day. There really is no polite way to say this: We live in a rude world. Rude, sarcastic remarks have become an accepted part of our everyday conversations. That's sad when we consider that rudeness shows *a lack of respect for another*. Rudeness hurts the person who is being disrespected, as well as the person who is failing to show respect.

First Peter 2:17 reminds us that we should respect everyone. Why? Because God made us all in His image. When we show respect for others, we are showing respect for the One who created us all. We see in Psalm 8:5: "Yet you [God] made them [men] inferior only to yourself; you crowned them with glory and honor" (GNT). Therefore, there are no worthless people! Everyone was created by God and is valued by Him, even those our society deems to be of little value. Calvary's Cross fully demonstrates the value that God places on every individual.

I once found myself dealing with a pharmacist who was extremely stressed and took it out on her customers, including this flu-ridden pastor. Feeling horrible, I didn't appreciate her attitude or her inability to have my medicine ready when it was promised. I was tempted to let her have a piece of my mind, but the Holy Spirit encouraged me to show her grace. When I finally had my medicine, I turned to leave and heard someone say, "Pastor Lynn, good to see you!" What a dismal witness my impatience would have been had I not remembered the importance of always showing others respect.

If grace-filled living is reflecting the character of Christ, then we should seek to love those whom He died to save. Treating *all* people with respect shows that we have personally experienced the love and grace of God, and we are willing to allow that love and grace to flow through our lives to touch the lives of others.

In his most famous speech, Martin Luther King, Jr. said: "I have a dream that my four little children will one day live in a nation where they will not be judged by the color of their skin, but by the content of their character." What a powerful vision! A person's character is not determined by nor should it be judged by the color of skin. Character can only be known as we develop friendships and get to know each other on the heart level.

In Romans 14:12–13, we are told: "So then, *each of us* will give an account of himself to God. Therefore let us stop passing judgment on one another. Instead, make up your mind not to put any stumbling block or obstacle in your brother's way" (NIV) (*emphasis added*).

As our self-consumed world becomes more and more crowded, as work-related stress levels continue to rise, as the complexities of life increase, rudeness will become more and more common. As grace-filled believers, our response to those in need should be one of courtesy and respect. I challenge you to quietly join the Polite Revolution, not for the sake of politeness, but because the Bible teaches us that *love is polite*. (See 1 Corinthians 13.)

When we face God's judgment day, we will be held accountable for how we treated one another. Let's go out and show a rude world what grace looks like. Let's become the Church Jesus Christ died for us to be.

SCRIPTURE
TO REMEMBER

Live wisely among those who are not believers, and make the most of every opportunity. Let your conversation be gracious and attractive so that you will have the right response for everyone.

—Colossians 4:5–6 NLT

QUESTION
?
OF THE
DAY

IN GRADE SCHOOL, WE ALL KNEW THAT "STICKS AND STONES MAY BREAK MY BONES, BUT WORDS WILL NEVER HURT ME." IN PROVERBS 15:4, WE READ: "GENTLE WORDS ARE A TREE OF LIFE; A DECEITFUL TONGUE CRUSHES THE SPIRIT" (NLT). WHICH OF THESE DO YOU BELIEVE TO BE TRUE? WHY?

_____

_____

" QUOTE, UNQUOTE "

Christianity is designed to refine and to soften; to take away the heart of stone, and to give us hearts of flesh; to polish off the rudeness and arrogances of our manners and tempers; and to make us blameless and harmless, the sons of God, without rebuke.

—John Jay

How can the Church begin a "politeness revolution"? What role can you play in such a revolution?

_____

_____

_____

_____

_____

_____

_____

_____

_____

_____

_____

_____

_____

_____

_____

_____

_____

_____

WHO'S IN CHARGE?

by Greg Kenerly

I was just out of college and serving in my first church as a youth pastor. Although I was twenty-two, I looked much younger, and I was even greener than I looked. I had a lot to learn about ministry—and life. So I was a bit surprised (and very excited) when I was placed in charge of an all-night youth event for about two hundred students at a local recreation center in our town. The recreation center had everything we would need for a successful event, including lots of outdoor space for teens to run around and have fun.

Unfortunately, the residents of the neighboring apartment complex were not nearly as excited as the teens and I were. Sometime around 2 a.m., a resident summoned the police to our event. When the officers arrived, I introduced myself as the person in charge. I could tell they weren't convinced that was true (I'm assuming because of my youthful looks). So they continued to work their way through the rec center, looking for an adult they could talk to. When they located one of the adult volunteers, he assured them I really was the person overseeing the event. The police officers finally spoke with me, we solved the problem at hand, and no one went to jail that night!

Thinking about that night makes me wonder: Can people clearly see that Christ is in control of my life? How about your life? Are people able to figure out who is in charge?

Unfortunately, many people who say they are followers of Jesus don't always live like it. I'm convinced that it's fairly easy to live the Christian life the vast majority of the time—let's say ninety-five percent. But it's during that other five percent, when we're facing the storms of life, that people watch us closely to see if we are living the same way we do when things are going well. They want to see who really is in charge of our lives. When small things don't go the way we would like them to—when someone cuts us off in traffic or our boss isn't exactly respectful or a classmate says something mean or hurtful—how we react shows us who really is in charge. The same is true when we face life's most challenging trials.

It's important that we live our lives in a way that demonstrates to others that Christ is leading us—not only when things are good, but especially during those difficult situations. When we react in a manner that is not a true reflection of Christ, it tarnishes our witness to those around us, and it also tarnishes the name of Christ to a world that is often looking for a reason to say, "I told you it's not real."

I believe that people deserve to see who Christ is through the positive and the negative circumstances of our lives as followers of Christ. So many times we tend to "take charge" when life gets difficult, but Matthew 5:16 reminds us that if we behave and react in a Christ-centered way, we will help others see who God really is and what He is like. It will help them draw closer to Him, as well.

So, who is in charge of your life? There's a lot riding on your answer.

SCRIPTURE
TO REMEMBER

"I said, 'You are my servant'; I have chosen you and have not rejected you. So do not fear, for I am with you; do not be dismayed, for I am your God. I will strengthen you and help you; I will uphold you with my righteous right hand."

—Isaiah 41:9b–10 NIV

" QUOTE, UNQUOTE "

Faith is a living and unshakable confidence, a belief in the grace of God so assured that a man would die a thousand deaths for its sake.

—Martin Luther

Write about a recent time when one of life's storms—big or small—hit your world. How did you react? Who was in charge? Would an outsider have agreed with your assessment?

TODAY'S PRAYER

Dear Lord, thank You for reminding me what is at stake. How I respond to storms may influence how others respond to You. Forgive me for the times I have taken charge of my life instead of giving it to You. I ask You to fully take charge in my life so that when I do face trials, I have Your protection and guidance, and those who see me will have hope in Your promises. In Jesus' name, amen.

In the world you face persecution. But take courage; I have conquered the world!

—John 16:33b NRSV

LET'S BE
COURAGEOUS

by Lynn Holmes

We all want to be heroes, and no one wants to be called a coward. In fact, cowardice is one of the most despised human qualities. Most of us will do almost anything to avoid being called a coward. Think back to when you were younger and school friends challenged you to do something dangerous with the ultimate dare: calling you a chicken!

Heroes, on the other hand, are the conquerors. They're the good guys. We've all seen the classic movies where the courageous good guys save the day, while the cowardly bad guys get what they have coming to them. All fathers want to be seen as heroes in the eyes of their spouses and children, the one who cares for and protects.

Among the courageous are those who rescue people from burning buildings, place themselves in the line of fire, and sacrifice for our freedoms. Also among the courageous are those who choose to be the faces of grace to others. It takes guts to stand up and do what's right, especially in a world that seems to value tolerance above all else. As truth is continually challenged, it seems fewer Christians are willing to stand up for their convictions. Some have even begun to doubt the existence of absolute right or wrong.

First Corinthians 16:13 challenges us to: "Be on guard. Stand firm in the faith. Be courageous. Be strong" (NLT). If we as Christ's followers recognize social ills, if we see immoral choices taking precedence over less-popular moral choices, if we see prejudicial treatment of our fellow man, we have a biblical mandate to take a stand for what is right and to let our love be seen. Ezekiel 3:18b exhorts us: "If you don't speak out to warn the wicked to stop their evil ways, they will die in their sin. But I will hold you responsible for their death" (NCV).

Read that again. In my eyes, it is one of the most sobering verses in the Bible. It tells me that if I know the truth—if God has shown me the difference between right and wrong—and I see somebody being mistreated or doing the wrong thing but do nothing about it, God will hold me responsible for my lack of obedience and my failure to take a stand.

This verse kept coming to mind when one of our church members, Dr. David Evans, told me his idea for producing a movie about grace and forgiveness. *The Grace Card* illustrates much-needed themes for our world. The story helps us discover that as believers in Christ Jesus, we can help end prejudice, heal bitterness, and demonstrate love and forgiveness in a way that draws people to God's grace—the only thing that can truly transform lives.

TAKE A STAND

The Bible teaches that when I know the difference between right and wrong yet I do nothing about it, I have indulged evil. What wrong can you begin to help right?

As we prayed about the idea of producing a movie, God reminded us that it would take courage to move forward. As a church, we believed God was leading us to make a strong statement to our society. We read in Psalm 119:41, 45–46: "Let your love, GOD, shape my life. ... Then I'll be able to stand up to mockery because I trusted your Word. ... And ... as I look for your truth and your wisdom; then I'll tell the world what I find, speak out boldly in public, unembarrassed" (MSG).

Not all of us are called to make a movie. Yet as believers, we are each called to courageously stand up for God's truth and share His grace lovingly with a world that is desperate for forgiveness. Anything less would be cowardly.

SCRIPTURE
TO REMEMBER

My brothers, as believers in our glorious Lord Jesus Christ, don't show favoritism. Suppose a man comes into your meeting wearing a gold ring and fine clothes, and a poor man in shabby clothes also comes in. If you show special attention to the man wearing fine clothes and say, "Here's a good seat for you," but say to the poor man, "You stand there" or "Sit on the floor by my feet," have you not discriminated among yourselves and become judges with evil thoughts?

—James 2:1–4 NIV

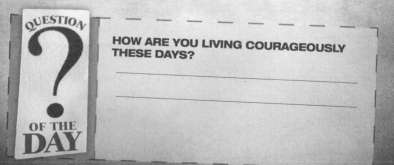

QUESTION
?
OF THE
DAY

HOW ARE YOU LIVING COURAGEOUSLY THESE DAYS?

_____

_____

Think of a person in your life who is being treated unfairly by others. What can you do to extend grace to that person today?

_____

_____

_____

_____

_____

_____

_____

_____

_____

_____

_____

_____

_____

_____

> *Do nothing out of selfish ambition or vain conceit,*
> *but in humility consider others better than yourselves.*
> *Each of you should look not only to your own interests, but*
> *also to the interests of others.*
>
> —Philippians 2:3–4 NIV

WARNING
SIGNS

by Greg Kenerly

We were in the middle of praying before our meal when Brian leaned over and whispered excitedly: "Jon!" After getting no response, Brian whispered again, but this time, he added a little more urgency to it: "Jon … *you're on fire!*" That got Jon's attention—and the attention of the rest of us in the crowded living room!

Jon had accidently backed up against a candle on the mantle and his shirt caught on fire without him knowing it. Once we realized what was happening, there was quite a flurry of activity. Fortunately, we extinguished the flames and Jon suffered no injuries. It was a story that we've laughed about often.

For Brian, it was easy to notice that Jon's shirt was on fire—the flames were a good indicator. Wouldn't it be helpful if God made things that obvious when someone around us is having a problem of some sort? What if a coworker—the guy who smiles and says everything is fine—came to work wearing a sign that said: *Help,*

I'm depressed and need a friend? You would know the truth and be better prepared to help him.

Or what if the cashier at the grocery store had a nametag that said: *I'm Sharon, my husband is an alcoholic and it's destroying our family*? You could talk to her about programs that serve families in this situation, and you could let her know you'll be praying for her. Or what about the kid in your classroom who seems to have it all together but is actually struggling with thoughts of suicide? What if he had a sign that said: *I'm not sure I'll be here tomorrow if something doesn't change today*? If that had happened when I was in high school, my friend Devin might still be around today.

His death came as a total shock because Devin seemed to have it together—outgoing, friendly, social. Although I was only in high school, I began to realize that we never know what someone is dealing with unless we're willing to be real. I decided then I would start listening to people, ask the hard questions, and be an encourager.

Since people don't wear signs, perhaps we should start paying closer attention. Not only to the people around us but also to the still, small voice of God. God knows what is going on inside the hearts and minds of people. And God is looking for those who are willing to make a difference in the lives of the hurting, confused, and discouraged people around us. The problem for many of us is that we are too busy and too preoccupied to focus on what God might be trying to say or what those around us might be struggling with.

TAKE A STAND

Too often, we think of prayer as passive. But it's a wonderful action step in serving others. Start now, lifting up to God those closest to you. As you continue through the day, ask God to help you pay attention to those you come in contact with, and be sure to pray for them as you interact.

I try to live by the old adage that God always has a plan, but He seldom carries it out alone. I believe God is looking for people to carry out those plans. Let's pay attention to the warning signs around us and to the call of God to help those in need.

If nobody in that room had been paying attention, Jon's shirt wouldn't have been the only thing to catch fire. Let's be a little more like Brian and become more aware of what is happening to those around us.

SCRIPTURE
TO REMEMBER

"Therefore everyone who hears these words of mine and puts them into practice is like a wise man who built his house on the rock. The rain came down, the streams rose, and the winds blew and beat against that house; yet it did not fall, because it had its foundation on the rock. But everyone who hears these words of mine and does not put them into practice is like a foolish man who built his house on sand. The rain came down, the streams rose, and the winds blew and beat against that house, and it fell with a great crash."

—Matthew 7:24–27 NIV

de•fin•ing moment

LISTEN: "TO GIVE ATTENTION WITH THE EAR; ATTEND CLOSELY FOR THE PURPOSE OF HEARING." HERE ARE FIVE WAYS YOU CAN BECOME A BETTER LISTENER: • TALK LESS, HEAR MORE. • LOOK PEOPLE IN THE EYE. • SEEK TO HEAR WHAT THEY ARE REALLY SAYING. • ASK QUESTIONS. • FOLLOW UP.

If you were wearing a sign, what would it say? Who do you know who might be trying to say something … if only someone were listening?

THE GRACE CARD
DVD-BASED STUDY

Experience a grace awakening with this four-week study!

THE GRACE CARD
DVD-BASED STUDY

is founded on life-changing, biblical principles of forgiveness and love. Engage in a four-week study using exclusive movie clips from *The Grace Card*, relevant Bible verses, questions for group discussion, and four thought-provoking Bible lessons.

This all-inclusive kit provides everything you need for individual or group study:

- DVD with *The Grace Card* movie clips for each lesson
- Study Guide that features an easy-to-use format, high-quality graphics, and Bible-based lessons
- Leader's Guide with tips for each lesson and instructions for leading a great small group

Look for *The Grace Card* **DVD-Based Study** at your local Christian bookstore, or visit **Outreach.com** for bulk quantities.

THE GRACE CARD STUDY GUIDE

Join a *Grace Card* study group and experience a grace awakening!

THE GRACE CARD STUDY GUIDE

integrates relevant Bible verses, inspired teaching, questions for group discussion, and four thought-provoking Bible lessons.

The Grace Card Study Guide includes four weekly sessions:

Grace Awakening: Experience freedom by giving and receiving God's grace.

Grace Overflowing: Transform your relationships through love and forgiveness.

Grace Lessons: Grow and mature spiritually through adversity, discipline, and God's Word.

Grace in Action: Change the world by extending God's grace.

The Grace Card **Study Guide** is written to be used with *The Grace Card* **DVD-based Study**, which features messages and movie clips from the film *The Grace Card*—a compelling story of two police officers who must somehow join forces to help one another in the face of bitterness, tragedy, and pain.

Look for *The Grace Card* **Study Guide** at your local Christian bookstore, or visit **Outreach.com** for bulk quantities.

I promise to pray for you,
ask your forgiveness, grant you the same,
and be your friend always.

....

I promise to pray for you,
ask your forgiveness, grant you the same,
and be your friend always.

....

I promise to pray for you,
ask your forgiveness, grant you the same,
and be your friend always.

....

I promise to pray for you,
ask your forgiveness, grant you the same,
and be your friend always.

....

I promise to pray for you,
ask your forgiveness, grant you the same,
and be your friend always.

....

I promise to pray for you,
ask your forgiveness, grant you the same,
and be your friend always.

....

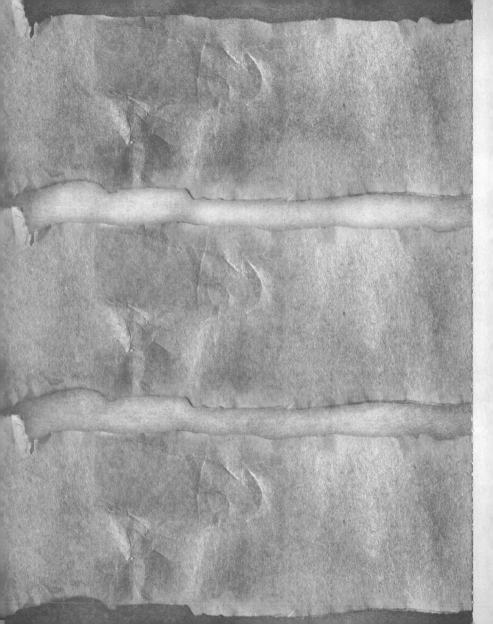